GOOD CLEAN FUN

GOOD CLEAN FUN

FIFTY NIFTY GAMES FOR JUNIOR HIGHERS

TOM FINLEY

Youth Specialties

ZONDERVAN PUBLISHING HOUSE
Grand Rapids, Michigan

i

GOOD CLEAN FUN: Fifty Nifty Games for Junior Highers

Youth Specialties Books are published by the Zondervan Publishing House
1415 Lake Drive, S.E., Grand Rapids, Michigan 49506

ISBN 0-310-31251-5

Edited by David Lambert

Illustrated by Tom Finley

Printed in the United States of America

86 87 88 89 90 91 / 10 9 8 7 6 5 4 3 2 1

Welcome to *Good Clean Fun!*—fifty nifty action-packed challenges and puzzlers wrapped around the Word of God.

Some of the games are easy. Some are very hard. But all are fun, and each will teach you something new about God's wisdom.

A few important notes: Most of the games require extra materials—pens, pencils, scissors, tape, or glue, for instance. And it's a good idea to grab some extra scratch paper for score keeping. Each game comes with a handy list of necessary materials.

Need copies for everybody in your group? No problem. Every page is reproducible on any photocopy machine. So run off as many copies as you need for your youth group activities or Bible studies. And feel free to modify any games or rules to suit your tastes.

In the back of the book you'll find an index of Bible verses used in the games. Here's a suggestion: when you and your friends are studying a portion of scripture, check that index to find out whether there's a game in this book that covers that scripture. If there is, play the game along with your study. Besides being fun, it will help you learn—and it will help you *retain* what you learn.

Oh, yes—the answers to the more difficult games are found in the "Answer Sheet" section at the back of the book. Now—enjoy some *GOOD CLEAN FUN!*

—Tom Finley—

Contents

Listed by game number, title, game type, subject, and key verse.

Salvation is found in no one else; for there is no other name under heaven given to men by which we must be saved.
———————————————————— *(Acts 4:12)* ————————————————————

This game may *look* easy, but wait till you try it. We call it

 **S.O.S.!**

- FOR ONE PLAYER
- MATERIALS NEEDED: Pencil and eraser. Optional: several sheets of tracing paper.
- INSTRUCTIONS: Here are six people in trouble. Your job is to rescue them by connecting each person with the proper rescuer. For example, you should connect the stranded astronaut to the space shuttle. *But*—you can never cross your path (except on pipes that go over or under the pipe you followed before) and you can never travel the same section of pipe twice. We suggest you use tracing paper, because chances are it will take you several tries.

Now that you've played the game, you have a pretty good idea what it takes to be saved or rescued—it takes a rescuer. The Bible verse above tells us that Jesus Christ is our rescuer. Now you know why people say that Jesus is the answer. He can answer our S.O.S.—He can Save Our Souls!

For solution, see Answer Sheet, page 104.

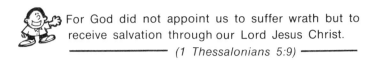 For God did not appoint us to suffer wrath but to receive salvation through our Lord Jesus Christ.

———————————— *(1 Thessalonians 5:9)* ————————————

Why do we need salvation? What is Christ saving us from? The answer is *sin*. Yep, sin cuts us off from God—and separation from God is the worst thing imaginable.

And speaking of separation, take a look at this little game we call

- FOR ONE PLAYER

- MATERIALS NEEDED: Pencil and eraser, Bible.

- INSTRUCTIONS: There are six little Bibles on the grid below. Each contains a thought about sin. There are also six bubbles, each of which contains a biblical reference. Here's your job: Use your Bible to look up the verses identified in the bubbles, then match them up with the Bible that summarizes the verse. Then use a pencil to connect each Bible with the corresponding bubble on the connecting black gridlines. But be careful! You can't use the same section of grid twice, and you can't cross your path.

Now that you've played the game: As you can see, each verse in the game has something important to say about sin and its effects. All people have sinned. Sin kills. Sin separates us from God. Now you know why we all need that salvation God gives to anyone who wants it!

For solution, see Answer Sheet, page 104.

I am the gate; whoever enters through me will be saved.
He will come in and go out, and find pasture.

——————————— (John 10:9) ———————————

Jesus is the door between God and humanity. But, according to the Bible, there is one thing Jesus expects of us before He allows us to pass through—one all-important *key* to the door. Do you know what that key is? You'll find out when you play

THE KEY TO THE KINGDOM!

- FOR ONE PLAYER

- MATERIALS NEEDED: Pencil or pen.

- INSTRUCTIONS: The answer will be revealed if you follow the proper path through the maze.

Now that you've found the key, would you like to know more? Read John 1:12; John 3:16; Romans 10:17; Romans 14:23; Ephesians 2:8; and Hebrews 11:1 and 6.

For solution, see Answer Sheet, page 104.

Faith isn't just optional for salvation—it's *necessary!* (See John 3:16; John 1:12). But what exactly *is* faith? Is it a vague feeling that, yes, some kind of god does live somewhere out in space? Is it the hope that if we're good enough, we'll make it to heaven?

Hmmm—sounds like we'd better find out exactly **WHAT IS FAITH?**

To find the answer, fold this page so that arrows A and B meet points A and B, as shown.

As a matter of fact, all the people above are more or less correct—faith *does* mean accepting something as true, it *is* relief from nagging doubts, and so on. But faith is much more than that, as you found out when you folded the page. What does the strange answer mean? It means that faith is putting *action* to your beliefs. Faith changes lives! And that means it changes more than just what you believe—it changes what you *do*—how you behave. If you have a true faith in Jesus Christ, your life will be radically changed over a period of time. Your old sinful ways will give way to a new Christ-centered life. Your belief must have feet.

WHO DO **YOU** THINK HE IS?

- FOR ONE OR MORE PLAYERS

- MATERIALS NEEDED: Pencil or pen.

Hoo, boy! Did we blow it! We wanted to do a game about many of the words that the Bible uses to describe Jesus Christ. You know, words like "Lord" and "Saviour." But in our mad rush to get to the printers, we dropped the words and broke them into bits! We tried to put them back together before our boss found out, but in our haste we mixed up all the words. Your job is to rearrange the words so that they make sense.

- INSTRUCTIONS: Split each word into two parts (not necessarily equal ones!), and then stick each front half together with the correct back half to find our original words. For example: "Gord" and "Wod" form "God" and "Word."

HINT: If you need help, look up these verses: John 1:14; Isaiah 9:6; John 14:6; John 10:11; John 1:41; John 10:9; 1 Corinthians 10:4; Luke 2:11; Matthew 21:11; Hebrews 12:24; John 1:29; John 8:12; Isaiah 9:6; and Luke 23:38.

Wock	Propiour	Gherd	Dong
Counth	Mediah	Trufe	Roy
Waiator	Laght	Kior	Lird
Shephet	Lid	Lormb	Savod
Messselor			

For solution, see Answer Sheet, page 104.

Who is this God who made everything? The Bible has much to say about Him—too much to put in this game! But we jammed in as much as would fit. Have fun unjamming!

WORD JAM!

● FOR ONE OR MORE PLAYERS

● MATERIALS NEEDED: Colored pencils, a different color for each player.

● INSTRUCTIONS: You've probably played this type of game before. To play it alone, just circle all the words you can find in the letter matrix on the next page that describe God. There are thirty-three. One is done as an example. The words are listed horizontally, vertically, and diagonally.

But for some *real* fun, play it with a friend or two. Here's how: When play begins, all players jump in and start to identify and circle words as fast as they can. The object is to find the most words. *But*—each letter in each word is worth one point. For example, "love" equals four points and "merciful" equals eight points. So the player who gets a lot of the bigger words will win! Incorrectly circled words are subtracted from a player's score.

FIND ALL THESE WORDS:

Almighty
Judge
Divine
Eternal
Spirit
Creator
Holy
Just
Righteous
Omniscience
Omnipotent

Omnipresent
Father
Perfect
Truth
Mercy
Corporeal
Invisible
Living
Good
Love
Benevolent

Rewarder
One
Glorious
Blessed
Wise
Powerful
Friend
Great
King
Light
Peace

Bible verses and definitions of the more difficult words are on page 104.

```
B E N E V O L E N T B C M N C C F R I E N D Z
X O B A L M I G H T Y I N C O R P O R E A L
G J M P E A C E O L G D K E G R E A T I S R
L U X N J Q K Z N A O R I P P A V T C E
O D S P I R I T Y T V O A A V N M M E T F G W
R G Q I K P H M O H E D A A X I G N R O H A
R N R G R S T E T E R N A L N E Z U S R R
I O A X V K H J E Z R Q J H G T H T E Z N T S B D
O U Y P I O M N I S C I E N C E O W W M H I L E
S T O S M M X J L E J S S P E R F E C T E R
L I V I N G H U I W N Q S I E E E Q R O H S W
T F G B T F A S G X Q T N K O N P C O E S I
U U X L B W U T H Y J M Q J K N K P Y W S E S
P O W E R F U L T Z O R I G H T E O U S S D E
```

God has poured out his love into our hearts by the Holy Spirit, whom he has given us.   *(Romans 5:5)*

Want to learn more about the Holy Spirit? Then play this crossword puzzle we call our

GOD'S WORD PUZZLE!

- FOR ONE PLAYER
- MATERIALS NEEDED: Pencil and eraser, Bible.

Important note: We've included Bible verses as hints. If you look them up, use a New American Standard Bible. A different version may contain slightly different words.

ACROSS:

1. He's the Spirit of God's _____ (child). Galatians 4:6

2. An underwater vessel.

5. How many thieves were crucified with Christ? Mark 15:27

7. One of the fruits of the Holy Spirit mentioned in Galatians 5:22.

13. The Spirit of _____ (purity). Romans 1:4

17. Present.

19. Sick.

20. Water from the eye.

22. The Spirit _____ us (causes us to contain as much as possible). Ephesians 5:18

24. One who makes. ("The Spirit of God has made me.") Job 33:4

25. The sons of God are all those who are _____ (guided) by the Holy Spirit. Romans 8:14

26. The Holy Spirit _____ (leads) Christ's disciples. John 16:13

29. A three- _____ play.

30. Jesus is the _____ (means of entrance) to salvation. John 10:9

31. Never play with a loaded _____.

32. The Holy Spirit will abide with us for _____ (always). John 14:16

33. He is the Spirit of _____ (ability to grasp the meaning of). Isaiah 11:2

34. Adam and _____. Genesis 3:20

35. One of the fruits of the spirit. Galatians 5:22

37. The sun, _____, and stars.

39. Pull.

40. In 2 Corinthians 3:18, the Spirit is called _____ (Master, ruler). Two words.

43. We shall be glorified in the twinkling of an _____. 1 Corinthians 15:52

44. Short for "south."

45. Past tense of "get."

46. He's the Spirit of _____ (opposite of death). Romans 8:2

47. By, near.

48. See.

50. The Spirit descended on Jesus as a _____ (white bird). Matthew 3:16

51. Faithful to someone.

56. Finish.

57. "You shall receive _____ (strength) when the Holy Spirit has come upon you." Acts 1:8

59. The Holy Spirit _____ (exalts with praise) Jesus. John 16:14

61. One of the fruits of the Spirit. Ephesians 4:4

63. "There is one body and _____ Spirit." Ephesians 4:4

DOWN:

1. One of the fruits of the Spirit in Galatians 5:23.

2. Rebellion against Christ. 1 Corinthians 8:12

3. Short for "United Nations."

4. Short for "Beryllium."

6. Us.

8. "We shall _____ (everyone) have to appear before the judgment seat of God." Romans 14:10

9. The Holy Spirit is _____ us. 1 Corinthians 6:19

10. "Create in me a _____ (purified) heart, O God." Psalm 51:10

11. She.

12. The Spirit is _____ (everlasting). Hebrews 9:14

13. An expression of laughter.

14. Commanded.

15. Not happy.

16. He is the Spirit of _____ (sound judgment). Isaiah 11:2

17. The land of milk and _____ (bee's liquid). Numbers 14:8

18. The Spirit is _____ (omnipresent). Psalm 139:7

21. Guy's name.

23. He is the Spirit of _____ (physical power). Isaiah 11:2

26. He is the Spirit of _____ (unmerited favor). Hebrews 10:29

27. The Spirit _____ (is located within) us. Romans 8:11

28. Too much wet paint will drip or _____.

31. One of the fruits of the Spirit in Galatians 5:23.

64. The Holy Spirit came upon David when he was anointed with _____ (viscous liquid). 1 Samuel 16:13

65. The Holy Spirit has _____ ed (cleansed) us in His name. 1 Corinthians 6:11

67. Accomplish, attain.

70. Short for "recreation vehicle."

71. One of the fruits of the Spirit in Galatians 5:22.

74. The _____ (pure, righteous) Spirit. Ephesians 1:13

76. One of the fruits of the Spirit in Galatians 5:22.

77. Short for "Save Our Souls."

78. Same as 56 across.

36. Not in.

38. One of the fruits of the Spirit in Galatians 5:22.

39. The Spirit convicts _____ of sin, righteousness, and judgment. Two words. John 16:8

41. Same as 34 across.

42. Replace the bottom of a shoe.

44. The Spirit _____ (encloses or identifies) us. Ephesians 4:30

49. Upon.

51. Satan is a liar and the father of _____ (untruths). John 8:44

52. Belonging to or possessed by.

53. Sound a dog makes.

54. First two vowels.

55. One of the fruits of the Spirit in Galatians 5:22.

58. Jealous of another's possessions. Mentioned in Romans 1:29.

59. He's the Spirit of _____ (supreme being). 1 Peter 4:14

60. The shortest distance between two points.

62. Expression of emotion or surprise.

66. Sound a dog makes.

68. Belonging to him.

69. Female person.

72. The Holy Spirit is _____ (enclosed by) us. 1 Corinthians 6:19

73. Refers to a singular object.

75. Upon.

For solution, see Answer Sheet, page 105.

"We will do everything the Lord has said; we will obey."
———————— (Exodus 24:7) ————

Here's a test of skills we call

★S·T·A·R·S. AND **STRIKES!**

- FOR TWO OR MORE PLAYERS

- MATERIALS NEEDED: One coin and pen or pencil to keep score.

Why do we usually like to do the same things our friends like to do? Because we enjoy hanging around with them, that's why! In the same way, people who love God want to hang around with Him and do what He wants to do.

On these pages you'll find several stars with Bible verses. The verses mention important things that God wants us to do. The circles, on the other hand, contain things only someone who is *very strange* would want to do!

INSTRUCTIONS: Place the top of these pages against the wall. Stand back a few feet. With a friend or two pitch your coin at the stars. When the coin touches any part of a star, that player receives ten points. If the player has actually done what the verse says—in the last twenty-four hours—that player earns an additional twenty points. But watch out! If the coin touches a circle, the player must do what the circle says, or lose *all* points! If the coin touches nothing, the player scores no points.

16

BE KIND

"Be kind to one another."
(Ephesians 4:32, NASB)

INTRODUCE
THE PLAYERS,
USING DONALD
DUCK'S VOICE!

FELLOWSHIP

"If we walk in
the light . . . we
have fellowship
with one another."
(1 John 1:7)

MAKE SIX
DIFFERENT
WEIRD FACES!

FAITH

"Stand firm in the faith."
(1 Corinthians 16:13)

BIBLE STUDY

"I have hidden
your word in
my heart."
(Psalm 119:11)

PRAYER

"Pray continually."
(1 Thessalonians 5:17)

RESIST
THE DEVIL

"Resist the devil
and he will
flee from you."
(James 4:7)

WEAR YOUR
SHOES ON THE
WRONG FEET!

SING
"I'M A LITTLE
TEAPOT, SHORT
AND STOUT"
WITH MOTIONS!

LOVE

"Do everything in love."
(1 Corinthians 16:14)

OBEDIENCE
TO GOD

"If you love Me,
you will obey
what I command."
(John 14:15)

17

Christians can talk to God anytime, anywhere, about anything at all.
That's why we call this game

HOTLINE TO *Heaven!*

● FOR ONE OR MORE PLAYERS

● MATERIALS NEEDED: Colored pencils, a different color for each player.

Little Earl is trying to place a long-distance call to God. Help him realize that it doesn't take a phone booth to strike up a conversation with the Lord!

INSTRUCTIONS: Starting at the telephone, find the route with the largest number of places to pray. End up in heaven. Award yourself one point for each place you find. You can play solitaire or with friends. Compare your score with the chart below.

There are two important rules: You can't use the same section of path twice, and you can't cross your own path, except on wires that don't touch. Of course, if you're playing with friends, each player gets to use any and all wires, regardless of what other players have done.

Prayer Chart

32—Lousy! Do it again!

33-35—Crummy! Try again!

36-38—Not bad for a *first* try!

39-40—That's more like it!

41—Good!

42—Great!

43-45—Hot stuff!

46+—Genius!

167 or more—Cheater!

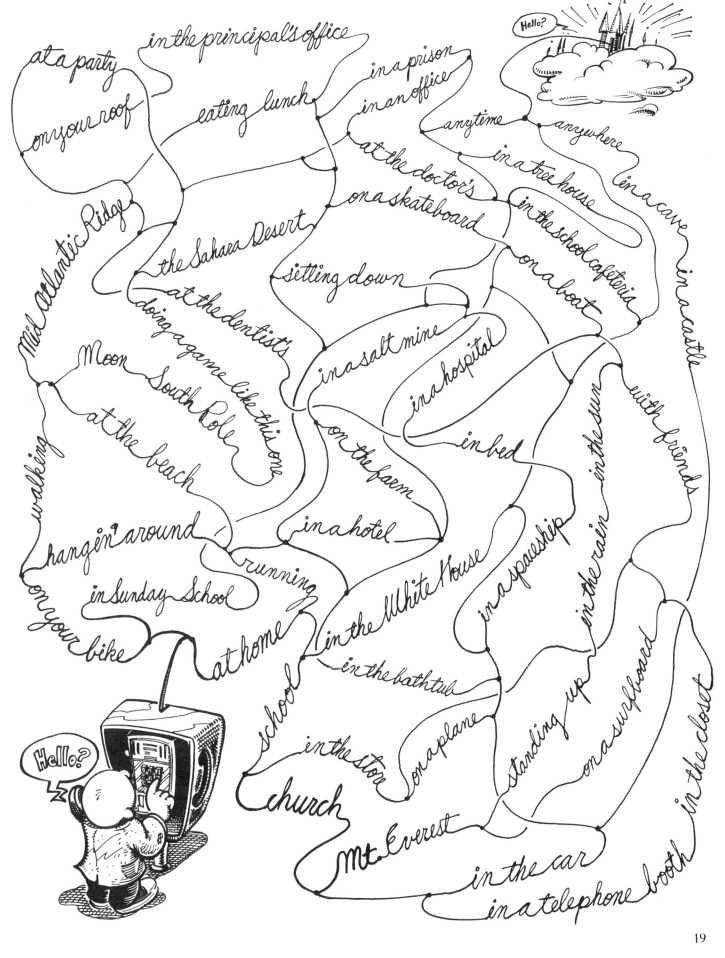

19

All Scripture is God-breathed and is useful for teaching, rebuking, correcting and training in righteousness, so that the man of God may be thoroughly equipped for every good work.   *(2 Timothy 3:16, 17)*

That Bible passage gives several good reasons for getting to know the Bible well. But if you're not familiar with the Bible, it may seem pretty large and scary at first!

Here's a challenging game that will help you take the important first step. We hope you enjoy

- FOR ONE PLAYER

- MATERIALS NEEDED: Pencil, Bible, and scratch paper

- INSTRUCTIONS: Take a look at this number star:

If you add up the four numbers in each straight line, you'll find that all five lines that form the star equal 56. For example, 2 + 13 + 30 + 11 = 56.

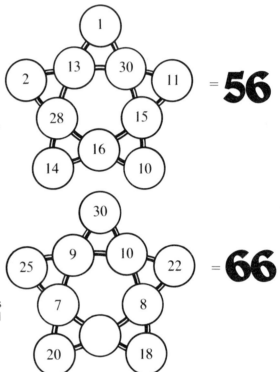

Now take a look at *this* number star:

In this case, each line adds up to 66. But one circle is empty. When playing number stars, the object of the game is to find the proper number for that circle so that all lines will add up to 66. In this star, the number is easy to find—it's 16. The game gets harder when there's more than one blank circle!

Now, to turn this game into *Bible Stars,* we've substituted books of the Bible for the numbers. If you look at the table of contents in your Bible, you'll see that Genesis is book number one, Exodus is two, and so on, up to Revelation, which is sixty-six. (Some versions of the Bible have additional books between the Old and New Testaments called the Apocrypha. To make things easier, we won't use or count those books in this game. Also, some versions may have different names for a few of the books. "Song of Solomon," for example, may be called "Song of Songs" in your Bible. For best results, use the New American Standard Version.) In the tables of contents of some Bibles, the numbers of the books are not given. If that's true of yours, you might want to write them in lightly in pencil before you play this game. You can erase them later, but it helps in playing *Bible Stars* to be able to see at a glance that Genesis is book one, First Kings is book eleven, Isaiah is book twenty-three, and so on.

OK, got it? Here's a typical Bible Star:

Bible stars work just like number stars, except that the numbers are the numbers of the Bible books shown on the star. For instance, the book at the top of the star is Ephesians—the forty-ninth book of the Bible. Below that and to the left is Genesis, the first book. Then comes Exodus, the second book, and at the bottom left is Second Kings, the twelfth book. Forty-nine plus one plus two plus twelve is sixty-four—in this star, the lines of the star all add up to *Third John,* which is the sixty-fourth book.

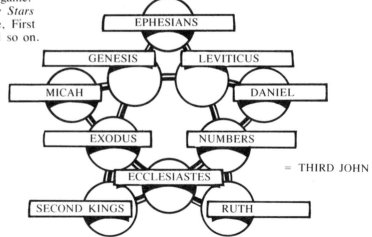

Play all the Bible stars listed here, and you'll remember the books of the Bible and their order better!

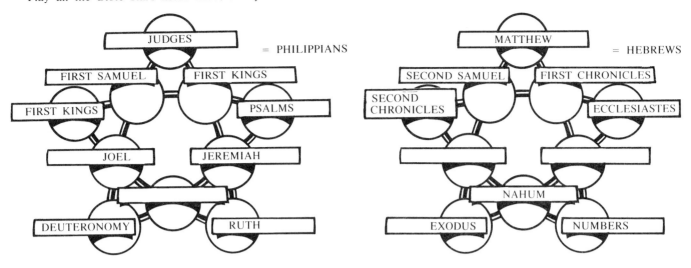

OK, ready for some *hard* ones? Here goes!

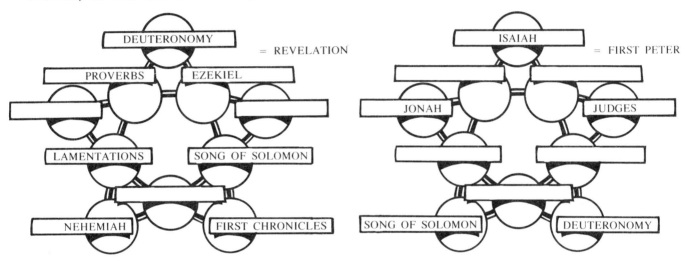

For those of you who are mathematical geniuses or at least extremely patient, here is the Bible star to end all Bible stars!

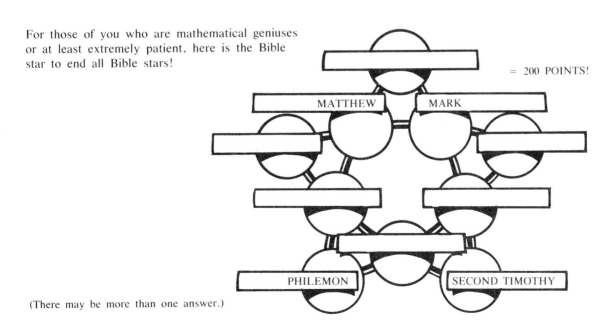

(There may be more than one answer.)

For solution, see Answer Sheet, page 105.

Let the word of Christ dwell in you richly.
——————————— (Colossians 3:16) ——

That's a smart idea! Christ's word is wisdom to live by.

Here's a simple game that will help you to learn the general order of the books of the New Testament—a good first step in gaining a handle on God's Word.

Since this game looks like a crossword puzzle, sort of, and because it concerns the word of Christ, we call it

CHRIST'S WORD PUZZLES!

- FOR ONE PLAYER

- MATERIALS REQUIRED: Pencil, eraser, and Bible or New Testament.

- INSTRUCTIONS: If you look at the sample game below, you can probably see what's going on here. First, you must figure out the names of those books of the New Testament numbered 1, 2, 3, 4, 5, and 26. (Count them in your Bible's table of contents. *Remember*—count only *New Testament* books.) Those books happen to be Matthew, Mark, Luke, John, Acts, and Jude. Once you figure that out, you must put them into the Christ's Word Puzzle grids so that they properly share letters. It's not hard—it just takes patience!

Sample game:

```
            L
      A   J U D E      Books 1, 2, 3, 4, 5, 26.
    M C     O K
  M A T T H E W
    R S     N
    K
```

Game one: Books 1, 9, 10, 19, 23, 25.

Game Two: Books 9, 10, 12, 13, 15, 16, 17, 19, 20, 21, 22, 23, 24, 25, 27.

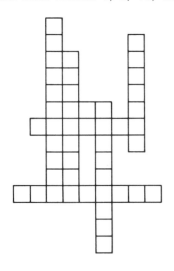

For solution, see Answer Sheet, page 105.

Do your best to present yourself to God as one approved, a workman who does not need to be ashamed and who correctly handles the word of truth.
—————————————— (2 Timothy 2:15) ——————————————

Here's a great card game that just might teach you something about the word of truth, the Bible. We call it

BIBLE BRIDGE!

- FOR TWO OR THREE PLAYERS. More can play if you use a copy machine to make an additional set of cards.

- MATERIALS NEEDED: Scissors, pencil or pen to keep score, Bible.

INSTRUCTIONS:

1. Cut out all thirty-six cards. Shuffle and deal six cards to each player. Place the remaining cards face down in a pile in the middle of the playing surface. Each card contains a Bible knowledge question, the Bible verse where the answer may be found, and a number (10, 20, or 30 points).

2. The object of the game is to score as few points as possible.

3. Players begin by picking up their cards. Each player chooses two cards to pass to the player on the left. Players should pass cards with difficult questions worth the most points. Players may not pass the two cards they just received.

4. When the players have passed cards, the player on the dealer's left chooses from his hand a card he thinks he knows the answer to. The card is placed face up for all to see. If the player's spoken answer is correct, the card is placed face down under the discard pile. If the answer is incorrect, the player returns the card to his or her hand and draws a card from the top of the discard pile. Use a Bible if no one is certain of the correct answer. Play goes to the left around the table.

5. The round is over when someone runs out of cards or there are no more cards in the discard pile. Players must add up the total points on the cards remaining in their hands.

6. Play ten rounds or so. Lowest final score is the winner.

Hint: Because there are two copies of each card, and because several rounds are played, it pays to listen to and remember the correct answers to the other players' cards. Next round, *you* may have to answer that question!

 USE THESE CARDS TO PLAY *BIBLE BRIDGE* AND *BIBLE CONCENTRATION*

God is now declaring that all men everywhere should _____.

(Acts 17:30)
10 points.

"The word of God is living and active and sharper than. . ."

(Hebrews 4:12)

Than what?
10 points.

"For there is one God and one _____ between God and men, the man Christ Jesus."

(1 Timothy 2:5)
10 points

"All have sinned and _____"

(Romans 3:23)
10 points.

The name "Jesus" (also called Immanuel) means:

(Matthew 1:23)
10 points.

"Draw near to God and. . ."

(James 4:8, NASB)

And what?
10 points.

What did God do because He loved the world?

(John 3:16)
10 points.

It is impossible to please the Lord without what?

(Hebrews 11:6)
10 points.

Christ was delivered up (crucified) for our _____ and was resurrected (raised from the dead) for our _____ _____.

(Romans 4:25)
20 points.

"The wages of sin is ____, but the gift of God is ____ in Christ Jesus our Lord."

(Romans 6:23)
20 points.

Those who ____ and ____ Jesus Christ receive the right to become children of God.

(John 1:12)
20 points.

Jesus said that He came to earth so that we might have ____ and have it _____.

(John 10:10)
20 points.

What, according to Jesus, are the two most important commandments?

(Matthew 22:37, 39)
20 points.

Name the nine fruits of the Spirit.

(Galatians 5:22, 23)
30 points.

"Here I am! I stand at the door and knock; if any one ____ and ____, I will ____ and eat with him, and he with me."

(Revelation 3:20)
30 points.

Matthew 28:19, 20 commands us to make ____ of all nations, ____ them in the name of the Father and the Son and the Holy Spirit, and ____ them to observe all Christ's commandments.

30 points.

"All Scripture is inspired by God and profitable for. . ."

(2 Timothy 3:16, NASB)

Name all four things mentioned in this verse. 30 points.

In order to fight Satan, Christians must wear the full armor of God. Name all six pieces of armor.

(Ephesians 6:14–17)
30 points.

28

God is now declaring that all men everywhere should ____.

(Acts 17:30)
10 points.

"The word of God is living and active and sharper than. . ."

(Hebrews 4:12)

Than what?
10 points.

"For there is one God and one ____ between God and men, the man Christ Jesus."

(1 Timothy 2:5)
10 points

"All have sinned and ____"

(Romans 3:23)
10 points.

The name "Jesus" (also called Immanuel) means:

(Matthew 1:23)
10 points.

"Draw near to God and. . ."

(James 4:8, NASB)

And what?
10 points.

What did God do because He loved the world?

(John 3:16)
10 points.

It is impossible to please the Lord without what?

(Hebrews 11:6)
10 points.

Christ was delivered up (crucified) for our ____ and was resurrected (raised from the dead) for our ____ ____.

(Romans 4:25)
20 points.

30

"The wages of sin is ____, but the gift of God is ____ in Christ Jesus our Lord."

(Romans 6:23)
20 points.

Those who ____ and ____ Jesus Christ receive the right to become children of God.

(John 1:12)
20 points.

Jesus said that He came to earth so that we might have ____ and have it _____.

(John 10:10)
20 points.

What, according to Jesus, are the two most important commandments?

(Matthew 22:37, 39)
20 points.

Name the nine fruits of the Spirit.

(Galatians 5:22, 23)
30 points.

"Here I am! I stand at the door and knock; if any one ____ and ____, I will ____ and eat with him, and he with me."

(Revelation 3:20)
30 points.

Matthew 28:19, 20 commands us to make ____ of all nations, ____ them in the name of the Father and the Son and the Holy Spirit, and ____ them to observe all Christ's commandments.

30 points.

"All Scripture is inspired by God and profitable for. . ."

(2 Timothy 3:16, NASB)

Name all four things mentioned in this verse.
30 points.

In order to fight Satan, Christians must wear the full armor of God. Name all six pieces of armor.

(Ephesians 6:14–17)
30 points.

Your word is a lamp to my feet and a light for my path.
——————————————— (Psalm 119:105) ———————

The better you get to know God's word, the easier it will be to cope with life. This simple game may teach you a few things about the Bible, or it may reinforce things you already know. Either way, we hope you will enjoy

BIBLE
CONCENTRATION!

- FOR TWO PLAYERS
- MATERIALS NEEDED: Scissors to cut out cards, Bible to check answers.

INSTRUCTIONS: Shuffle the cards and lay them face down on the floor or table in a six-by-six grid, as shown.

A player turns up two cards. If they match—*and* if the player can answer the question correctly—then the player picks up and keeps the two cards and takes another turn. If he can't answer the question, or if the two cards don't match, the cards are replaced face down. The other player can then try to choose two matching cards.

When all the cards are gone, the player with the most cards is the winner.

And let us consider how to stimulate one another to love and good deeds,
not forsaking our own assembling together, as is the habit of some, but encouraging
one another; and all the more, as you see the day drawing near.

——————————— (Hebrews 10:24, 25, NASB) ———————————

That "assembling together" is what we call the local church. In a sense, each Christian member is like a piece of a picture puzzle. When all the pieces are assembled the picture is whole.

Why should we meet together? For many reasons, as you'll see when you try your hand at

----------- THE CHURCH SEARCH! -----------

- FOR ONE PLAYER
- MATERIALS NEEDED: Scissors and pencil or pen.

INSTRUCTIONS: This is a typical word search puzzle, but with a twist. Your job is to find, in the letter grid, all twelve words and phrases listed below and circle them. The problem is that all nine pieces of the letter grid must be assembled together, and they must be fitted together properly. Otherwise, you won't be able to find all the purposes. Hey! That sounds kind of like the local Christian church! If you or a few others aren't there and aren't fitted in properly, the church just isn't what it could be!

The words and phrases run horizontally and vertically. They also twist and turn!

PURPOSES OF THE LOCAL GROUP OF CHRISTIAN BELIEVERS:

1. *Fellowship* (1 John 1:3) Fellowship includes friendship, fun, and unity.
2. *To evangelize the community* (Acts 1:8) Evangelize means to tell others about Christ.
3. *To glorify God* (Ephesians 3:21)
4. *Service to God and to man* (Ephesians 4:12)
5. *Unity* (Ephesians 4:13)
6. *Bring believers to maturity* (Ephesians 4:13)
7. *Building up in love* (Ephesians 4:16)
8. *To help its members improve* (1 Corinthians 14:26)
9. *To purify believers* (Ephesians 5:23-27)
10. *Christian education* (Ephesians 4:11–12)
11. *To encourage all to love* (Hebrews 10:24)
12. *To do good* (Hebrews 10:24)

```
A E U N T X Z R
J V P B H I E T
E E I C H R I S
E S R N L O V E U
S R N L O V E U
I S T O M A T U
```

```
E L I E V E R S
N C O U R A G E
B E R S E E A A
Y E A I E V T L
T H Y M N E H L
```

```
G G L M I E N I
B B D L T O G L
T E I W O S E R
T L N S Y O L E
O I G E E N I T
```

```
P U R I F Y B
S H I P T O E
P I T S M E M
R S E G I B T
A N O R B L O
```

```
B L O O V E T O
I B F E L L O W
O R B T O H E L
D I U X O Y V O
U N I T Y M A V
```

```
U N N I K T D
H E C O M M U
T I A N E D U
N I F I E E D
R I T Y J E S
```

```
E E D P D R U T
D O N R U Y R O
O D A O R O E L
I F N V B M T O
A I D E Y E O V
```

```
I A N D T O D
O R I F Y G O
V I C E T O G
A R L Y J E O
O B E O R N O
```

```
X X T O M A N E
N I T Y G A V B
C A T I O N B B
O R B I L L O T
U Z O Y O U R T
```

There are many other purposes we could have put in this game. But these ought to give you a good start! Attend church! Be involved.

For solution, see Answer Sheet, page 106.

Now may the God who gives perseverance and encouragement grant you to be of the same mind with one another according to Christ Jesus; that with one accord you may with one voice glorify the God and Father of our Lord Jesus Christ.

——————————— *(Romans 15:5, 6, NASB)* ———————————

There are fat Christians, there are thin Christians, pretty ones, ugly ones, smart ones, dumb . . . well, the list goes on forever because all Christians are people, and all people are different. Yet the Bible passage above indicates that we Christians should be of the same mind. There is a word that describes what that means. You can find it if you put together this jigsaw puzzle we call

PEOPLE ARE PUZZLING!

- FOR ONE PLAYER.
- MATERIALS NEEDED: Scissors.
- INSTRUCTIONS: These very strange people have just shown up at your church! After the initial shock wears off, you decide to help them fit in. Carefully cut each person out and assemble them together to make a unified whole. Big hint: the puzzle has holes in it!

For solution, see Answer Sheet, page 106.

For all have sinned and fallen short of the glory of God.
———————————— (Romans 3:23) ————————————

LOVE   Safety Net Targets

JOY   PEACE

PATIENCE

This verse is one of the best-known and most important ones in the Bible. But do you know what it means? Just exactly what *is* sin? Tell you what—we'll take a shot at explaining it to you if you'll take a shot at

KINDNESS

HUMAN CANNONBALL!

- FOR ONE OR MORE PLAYERS

GOODNESS

- MATERIALS NEEDED: Pencil.

FAITHFULNESS

INSTRUCTIONS: The verse tells us that sin is falling short of what God wants. OK—let's play a game where "falling short" is just what you *don't* want to do!

GENTLENESS

Put the point of your pencil on the Human Cannonball's nose. Close your eyes and, in one simple motion, move your pencil to one of the safety net targets. Open your eyes. Did you land in the net, or is the Human Cannonball's day ruined? If you missed the mark, you sinned! Give yourself ten points for a hit, subtract five points for a miss. Try to hit all nine nets in turn.

SELF-CONTROL

The safety nets represent some of the many good things God would like to see in your life. They are mentioned in Galatians 5:22, 23.

BOOM! YAAAA!

Human Cannonball

Did you do a lot of *sinning* during this game? That is—did you fall short of the target? Remember, sin is missing God's best. The Human Cannonball can explain the *impact* of that!

No temptation has seized you except what is common to man. And God is faithful; he will not let you be tempted beyond what you can bear. But when you are tempted, he will also provide a way out so that you can stand up under it. *(1 Corinthians 10:13)*

In the South American jungles, tribesmen use a strange device to trap monkeys alive for zoos and medical researchers. It's a hollowed—out coconut chained to a tree. The coconut has a monkey-hand-size hole in it. In full view of the monkeys, a tribesman will drop a piece of bait—candy or food—into the hole. Later, a foolish monkey will reach in and grab the bait. . .and discover that his fist is too big to take out! Believe it or not, that dumb monkey will sit there chained to the tree only by his stupidity until the tribesmen return to catch him. It works every time.

Temptation is like that piece of candy. Reach for it—and you find that you're in a sin trap just waiting for Satan to come take you away.

So how about it? Are you smart enough to simply let go of your sin and run away? Or are you a dumb monkey chained to a tree? Find out when you play

FOR TWO TO THREE MONKEYS—ER, PLAYERS.

MATERIALS NEEDED: Scissors to cut out cards. Cardboard, glue, or tape, and pencil to make spinner.

INSTRUCTIONS: A monkey with any brains would know how to escape a monkey trap. But these monkeys have no brains. Your job is to get some brains for your monkey.

1. Cut out and assemble spinner as shown.
2. Cut out all the Monkey Cards and Brains Cards.
3. Give each player three Monkey Cards. Put the Brains Cards in a pile on the board.
4. Object of the game is to be the first player to move all three of his monkeys into the Freedom area.
5. Players take turns spinning the spinner and moving one of their monkeys the appropriate number of spaces. Each player has only *one* of his monkeys in play at a time.
6. As soon as a monkey reaches the Freedom area, that player takes one Brains Card and starts another monkey on his next turn.
7. Along the trail there are several "Monkey Trap!" squares and "Brains" squares. If a monkey lands on a "Brains" square, that player takes a Brains Card. If a monkey lands on a "Monkey Trap!" square, that monkey is trapped until one of two things happens: If the player has a Brains Card, the player can place the card on the trapped monkey. That monkey is now free, and can be moved on that player's next turn. The Brains Card is returned to the pile. Or, if the player does *not* have a Brains Card, he must start a new monkey and hope it lands on a "Brains" square to gain the needed card. If it does, the trapped monkey may be freed with that card—but, since only one monkey can be in play at a time, the newly freed monkey must return to the beginning and wait its turn.
8. No two monkeys can occupy the same square or trap at the same time. If a monkey lands on an occupied square, return it to the square it was on before and lose that turn.
9. If no player has three surviving monkeys, the game is over—no one wins!.

Monkey 1	Monkey 2	Monkey 3	Brains Card	Brains Card	Brains Card	Brains Card	Brains Card
Monkey 1	Monkey 2	Monkey 3	Brains Card	Brains Card	Brains Card	Brains Card	Brains Card
Monkey 1	Monkey 2	Monkey 3	Brains Card	Brains Card	Brains Card	Brains Card	Brains Card

Freedom!

Congratulations! By letting go of all your sin traps, you are free!

In real life you can escape sin by letting go of it and avoiding it. For example, if you blow it by drinking at parties . . . avoid drinking parties! It takes only half a brain to see that! Don't let sin make a monkey out of you!

Glue or tape this spinner to cardboard. Jam the pencil through the center as shown. Spin the spinner like a top and let it fall. Whichever number is on top is the number of spaces to move.

"For I will forgive their wickedness, and will remember their sins no more."

(Hebrews 8:12)

HOW MANY SINS DOES GOD REMEMBER?

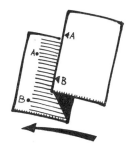

To find the answer to this important question, fold in this page so that arrows A and B meet points A and B as shown.

A •   ◀ B

A •   ◀ B

How can we be sure God will forgive our sins? Read and follow God's advice:

"If we confess our sins, he is faithful and just and will forgive us our sins and purify us from all unrighteousness." (1 John 1:9)

God is now declaring to men that all everywhere should repent, because He has fixed a day in which He will judge the world.

——————————————— (Acts 17:30, 31, NASB) ———————

There is more rejoicing in heaven over one sinner who repents than over ninety-nine righteous persons who do not need to repent.

——————————————— (Luke 15:7) ———————————

"Repent" is one of those Bible words that nobody uses in everyday conversation. But it's still an important word—even to *you*. So you should know exactly what it means. How can you find out? You guessed it! Play **LOADS OF CODES!**

- FOR ONE PLAYER
- MATERIALS NEEDED: Pencil or pen.
- INSTRUCTIONS: Work this word picture puzzle. It will tell you what to do next.

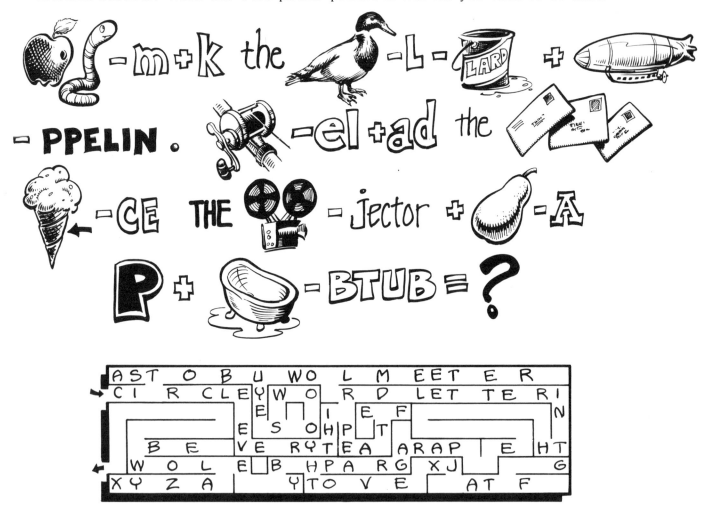

And I was showing fear. But I was not so we rose. Can I taste the hair? I Believe. Eat the cod.

(List the paragraph's decoded message here.) ___ ___ ___ ___ ___ ___,

___ ___ ___ ___ ___ ___, ___ ___ ___ ___ ___ ___ ___ ___ ___,

___ ___ ___.

Decode the clues below using the code revealed in the paragraph above. When you've decoded the crossword's clues, fill in the clues' answers on the puzzle grid. The shaded squares will spell out the final message, the definition of "repent." (If you did everything right!)

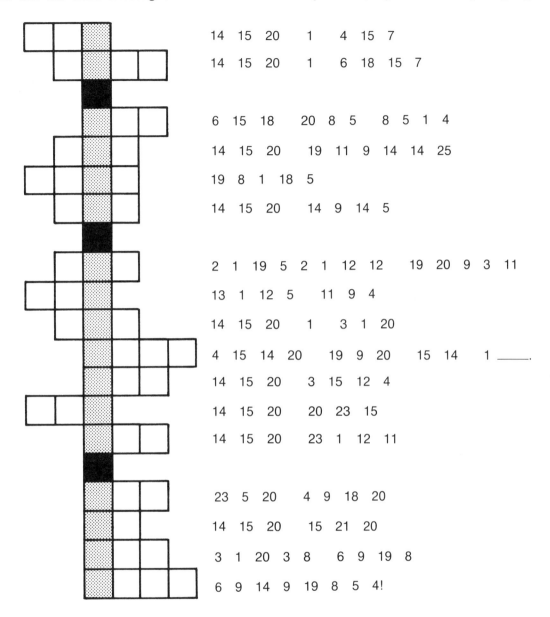

14 15 20   1   4 15 7

14 15 20   1   6 18 15 7

6 15 18   20 8 5   8 5 1 4

14 15 20   19 11 9 14 14 25

19 8 1 18 5

14 15 20   14 9 14 5

2 1 19 5 2 1 12 12   19 20 9 3 11

13 1 12 5   11 9 4

14 15 20   1   3 1 20

4 15 14 20   19 9 20   15 14   1 _____.

14 15 20   3 15 12 4

14 15 20   20 23 15

14 15 20   23 1 12 11

23 5 20   4 9 18 20

14 15 20   15 21 20

3 1 20 3 8   6 9 19 8

6 9 14 9 19 8 5 4!

Did you work the codes correctly? Do you understand what the message means? It means that when we ask God to forgive our sin, He expects us to change how we think about that sin. He wants us to hate it as much as He does.

"Repent" also means "turn back." That means simply that when we sin, we are in effect walking away from God. He wants us to turn back and walk with Him.

For solution, see Answer Sheet, page 106.

He who doubts is like a wave of the sea, blown and tossed by the wind.

(James 1:6)

Everyone has doubts now and then—questions about the Bible, worries about God, and so on.

There is only one way to deal with doubts. Face them head on and take them directly to God. Discuss your doubts with someone who can help you. If you hide your little doubts away, they'll grow into big problems. Deal with your doubts before they chew you up! So—if you don't doubt what we say, get ready for a fun game we call

DOUBT SHARKS!

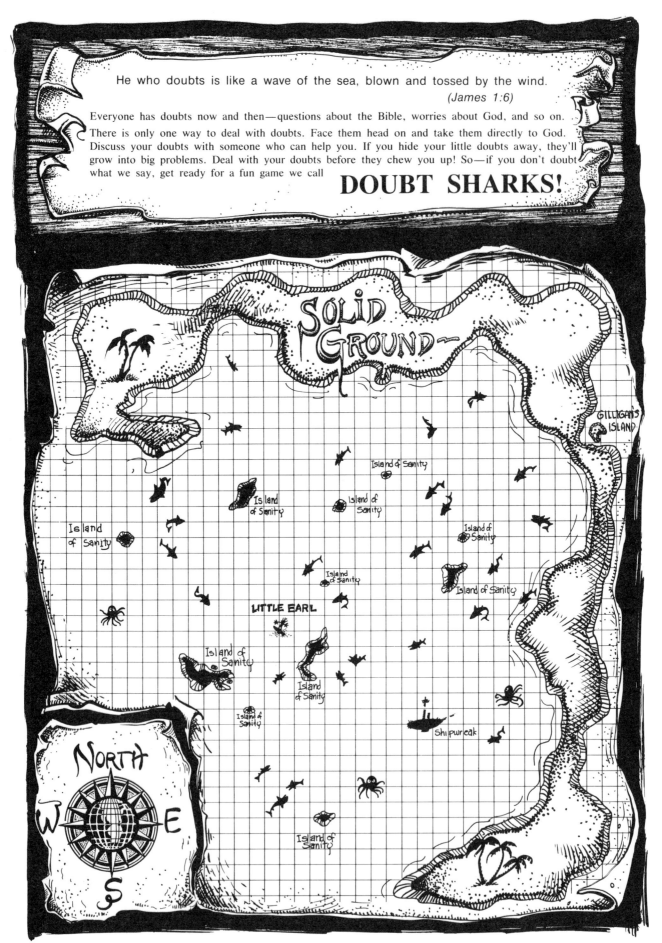

- FOR ONE OR TWO PLAYERS

- MATERIAL NEEDED: Scissors, glue or tape, and pencil for spinner, two pencils of different colors for two players.

- INSTRUCTIONS: Little Earl has decided to go surfing. Not knowing anything about surfing, Earl finds that he's been driven by waves and tossed by the wind far away from Solid Ground. Your job is to help him find his way through hazardous waters to home.

1. Cut out and assemble the spinner as shown.
2. Cut out the twelve Bible Cards. Give each player four cards and put the rest in a pile. This game can be played by one or two players. The rules remain the same.
3. First player spins the spinner. The player puts his or her pencil on Little Earl and draws a line as indicated by the spinner. For instance, if the spinner says "2 North," draw a line two grid spaces north. The directions are shown on the compass. Players take turns, each player creating his or her individual path.
4. The object is to be the first to draw a line leading Little Earl to Solid Ground.
5. But the Doubt Sharks and other hazards are in the way. If a player's line lands on or crosses a shark or other obstacle, that player is wounded. After three wounds, a player is dead and must start over at the beginning.
6. *But*—a player can escape from the hazard without being wounded if he plays a Bible Card. A card is played simply by reading its verse out loud and then putting the card under the pile.
7. If a player's line touches the edge of the map, that player has fallen off the world and must start over at the beginning! If a player has a Bible Card when he falls off the world, he may put his card under the pile and start again at any Island of Sanity he chooses.
8. A new card can be drawn every time a player's line lands on or crosses an Island of Sanity—*except* if he is on the Island because he has just fallen off the world. Of course, if all cards have been drawn from the pile, it is not possible to draw a card.

Glue or tape this spinner to cardboard. Jam the pencil through the center as shown. Spin the spinner like a top and let it fall. Whichever direction is on top is the course to follow.

Bible Cards:

Do not let your hearts be troubled. Trust in God; trust also in me. (John 14:1)	Take up the shield of of faith, with which you can extinguish all the flaming arrows of the evil one. (Ephesians 6:16)	Fight the good fight of the faith. (1 Timothy 6:12)	Who is it that overcomes the world? Only he who believes that Jesus is the Son of God. (1 John 5:5)
Faith comes from hearing the message, and the message is heard through the word of Christ. (Romans 10:17)	Put on the breastplate of faith. (1 Thessalonians 5:8, NASB)	Let us fix our eyes on Jesus, the author and perfecter of our faith. (Hebrews 12:2)	This is the victory that has overcome the world, even our faith. (1 John 5:4)
We live by faith, not by sight. (2 Corinthians 5:7)	But the Lord is faithful, and He will strengthen and protect you from the evil one. (2 Thessalonians 3:3)	The testing of your faith develops perseverance. (James 1:3)	Be on your guard; stand firm in the faith; be men of courage; be strong. (1 Corinthians 16:13)

Now that you've played the game: Faith is like any skill. It takes time and practice to build it up to full strength. If you face a doubt or have a question, seek help from your youth minister or other respected Christian. Each time a doubt is conquered, it makes you stronger!

Do you not know? Have you not heard? The Lord is the everlasting God, the Creator of the ends of the earth. He will not grow tired or weary, and his understanding no one can fathom.   *(Isaiah 40:28)*

God is infinite. What does that mean? It means, for one thing, that it will take an eternity to learn everything about Him. Getting to know God is almost like putting together a huge picture puzzle: It takes great patience and some effort, but each time a new piece is fitted in it brings a sense of joy and triumph.

Here is a simple jigsaw puzzle with a twist—it can be assembled in two completely different ways! You see it below assembled so that it spells "God." To learn a very important characteristic of God, play

A PUZZLING GOD?

- FOR ONE PLAYER

- MATERIALS NEEDED: Scissors.

- INSTRUCTIONS: Cut the puzzle apart and rebuild it to form a new word. That word is the foundation of God's relationship to humanity! Hint: When reassembled, the puzzle will be exactly the same size and shape it originally was. And you don't need to turn any pieces over.

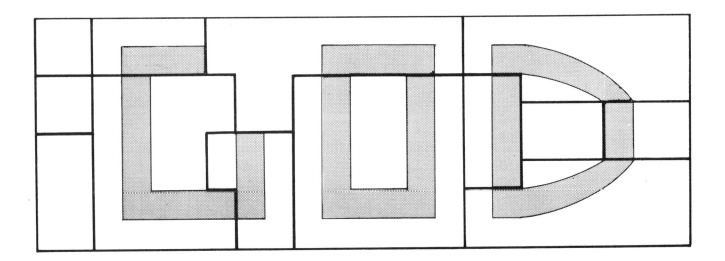

For solution, see Answer Sheet, page 106.

"All men will know that you are my disciples if you love one another."
— *(John 13:35)* —

We all know that God is the source of love. But do you know that God wants you to reflect His love to those around you? You are a sort of mirror, reflecting God's love into a dark world.

Try this simple project we call **MIRROR OF LOVE!**

- FOR ONE PLAYER

- MATERIALS NEEDED: Scissors, pencil, and wall mirror. Optional: Glue and black cardboard.

- INSTRUCTIONS:

1. Cut out the wheel (Be sure to cut out all ten slots, too!) and stick a pencil through the center. Optional: Glue the wheel to black cardboard for more durability. It's important that the rear of the wheel be black.

2. As you look directly at the wheel, spin it rapidly with the pencil. What happens? The image blurs into a gray sludge. Useless!

3. Now point the image on the wheel at a mirror and spin the wheel. As you spin the wheel, look into the mirror by looking through the slots as shown. *Ta da!*

You see, without the reflecting mirror, the image was a hopeless, uninteresting blur. But the mirror brought the image into sharp focus.

Are your friends uninterested in God? That may be because they have never been touched by His love. You be the mirror. Reflect His love into the lives of people you know.

Die for a friend? Wow! That's quite a friendship! Would you die for a friend? In fact, what are the limits on your friendship? A good way to find out is to compare yourself to

A FRIEND *INDEED!*

- FOR ONE OR MORE PLAYERS

- MATERIALS NEEDED: Scissors.

INSTRUCTIONS: The cards below list eight things that someone might do for a friend. Some are pretty serious—and some are pretty crazy! Cut the cards out. Shuffle all the *1* cards and place them face down in a pile. Do the same for the *2* and *3* cards, so that you have three separate stacks. Now draw one card from each stack and place them in numerical order: 1, 2, 3. They'll make a sentence—read it to see what sort of friend you might be. There are 512 possible combinations.

1	2	3	1	2	3
I'd run in front of a speeding	truck	to save your life.	I'd give you my last	shirt	to keep you warm.
I'd use your	toothbrush	to brush my teeth.	I'd race into a burning	house	to rescue you.
I'd let you use my	comb	to comb your greasy hair.	I'd let you cry on my	shoulder	to make you feel better.
I'd date your	ugly cousin	to make your mother happy.	I'd lend you my favorite	handkerchief	to wipe your nose on.

"But God demonstrates His own love for us in this: While we were still sinners, Christ died for us.
(Romans 5:8)

Jesus demonstrated that His love has no limits. He willingly lay down his life to save ours. Is Jesus your friend? He told us how to be His friend in these simple instructions: "You are my friends if you do what I command." (John 15:14)

51

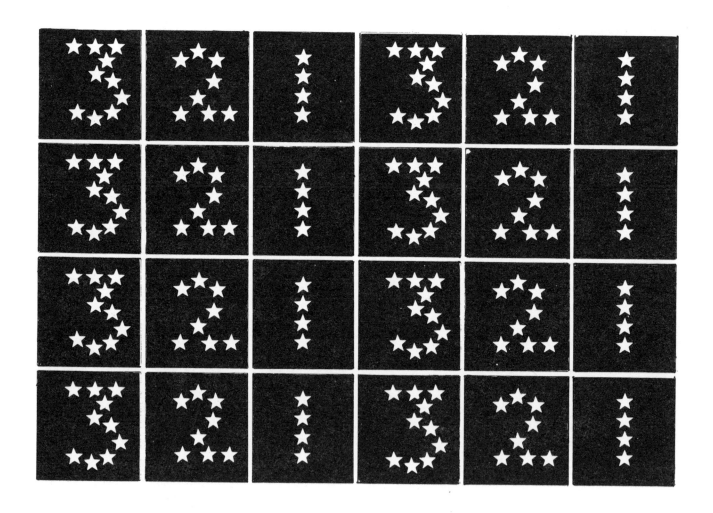

And what kinds of commands does Jesus give? Not a list of "dont's," but rather a lifetime of meaningful responsibilities. In other words, Christ gives us purpose in life; a reason to be alive. We Christians are here to make a difference in this world. And believe it, the world desperately needs us!

If you don't believe that (or even if you do), play

EARTH COMMAND!

- FOR ONE PLAYER
- MATERIALS NEEDED: Pencil or pen.
- INSTRUCTIONS: The earth is flying through dangerous days. There are some *big* problems—the threat of nuclear war, nationwide famines, poverty, political death squads, violence in the streets, and of course spiritual separation from God's love. And there are problems like lonely people in your class, kids on alcohol or drugs, and so on. You, as a representative of Jesus Christ here on earth, may be able to make a difference. It's not hard. All you have to do is follow Christ's commands. He'll take care of the rest. Some examples of His commands are written in this maze. As long as you follow the commands, you'll be on the right path.

Now that you've played the game: The maze was pretty easy, right? That's because you followed God's Word. His wisdom and instructions were your guide. It's the same in real life, of course. You'll make it through, and help others too, if you walk with the Lord.

53

Sounds like we'd better find out what God's will is and start doing it! But sometimes it seems as if God's will is somewhere way out in space—hard to know. Is there a way we can find God's will? The answer is on the space ship's view screen on the opposite page. Help the Astronavigator Pilot find the answer by playing

WHERE THERE'S A WILL, THERE'S A WAY!

- FOR ONE PLAYER

- MATERIALS NEEDED: pencil or pen (a brightly colored felt pen would be best).

- INSTRUCTIONS: The Astronavigator can find the answer if you'll help him follow the correct route. As you can see, the view screen has a grid marked with the directions "Up," "Down," "Left," and "Right." Put the point of your pen or pencil on the star named "Arcturus" and draw a single line according to the directions printed in the "Astronavigator Pilot's Star Catalog."

Now that you've finished the game: You probably said, "Hey, I knew that all the time." (If you can't figure out the answer, you either need to check your accuracy or take a closer look at the map.) If you are interested in some verses that spell out God's will, read:

John 6:40—eternal life.

Galatians 1:4—delivery from an evil age.

Ephesians 1:5—we've been adopted.

1 Thessalonians 5:18—be thankful.

1 Timothy 2:4—salvation and knowledge.

ASTRONAVIGATOR PILOT'S STAR CATALOGUE

Number of grid spaces to move:

2 left (This has been drawn on the screen as an example.)

		1 down
	1 down	1 left
3 down	1 right	1 down
2 right	1 down	1 right
2 down	1 right	1 down
2 left	3 down	1 right
4 down	1 left	3 down
3 right	1 down	1 left
2 down	1 left	1 down
2 right	1 down	1 left
2 down	3 right	1 down
32 left	13 up	3 right
2 up	2 right	13 up
2 right	13 down	2 right
13 up	1 right	11 down
4 right	13 up	3 right
1 down	4 right	2 down
1 right	1 down	1 right
1 down	1 right	13 up
1 right	1 down	5 right
3 down	1 right	2 down
1 left	3 down	1 left
1 down	1 left	
1 left		

Hebrews 10:10—sanctification (being set apart for a special purpose).

1 Peter 2:15—our good deeds will silence disbelievers.

Read these verses! After all, it should make you very happy to know that these nice things and many more are God's will for you. Remember, the Bible contains principles to live by. Let God's Word be your guide.

For solution, see Answer Sheet, page 106.

Serve one another in love.
—————(Galatians 5:13)—

In other words, God wants us to show our love by *doing* things, rather than just flappin' our gums! So, what sort of things can we do? You'll find out if you play

- FOR ONE PLAYER
- MATERIALS NEEDED: Pencil

ACROSS: _____

1. Make _____ (pay calls) to the old folks home with your youth group.
6. Say _____ (hello) to someone with a phone call.
8. Visit people _____ (contained by) jail.
11. Start a _____ (Scripture research) at your school. Two words.
14. Share your _____ (frozen water) cream.
16. _____ (cease to blame or require payment) someone.
18. Take a friend to Walt Disney's _____ Center.
19. Not appropriate.
21. Short for "General Electric."
22. Tell your friends about Jesus.
25. An Old Testament Hebrew name for God.
26. Wish someone _____ (Merry Christmas).
29. Road paving.
30. Visit someone in the _____ (medical institution).
33. Short for "Roxanne."

35. Another word for "Huh."
36. Have a heart of _____ (gold chemical symbol).
37. Serve someone a _____ (very warm) meal.
38. _____ (pluck) flowers for your mom.
39. Jacob's brother.
41. Way for travel.
43. An exciting feeling.
45. Nice looking.
47. Material.
50. _____ (ask) someone to church.
54. Short for "Ontario."
55. Unusual.
57. Don't let this get the better of you.
58. Be this to a fault.
61. Short for "Multiple Sclerosis."
63. Visit the _____ (ill).
65. Et cetera.

56

66. Digestive tract.
67. Hawaiian Island.
69. What you might hear in an elevator. Two words.
72. _____ (to make glad) up a friend.
74. _____ (clear of mess) your room without being told.
75. Never _____ (spread stories).

76. An expression of surprise.
77. In a place.
78. Unhappy.
79. Expression of fear, plural.
80. Same as 77 across.
81. Male offspring.
82. Run a high temperature.
83. _____ (remain) with a sick friend.

DOWN: _____

1. _____ (offer to serve) to help around your church.
2. Give time or money to those who _____ (experience stress).
3. Sour.
4. _____ (be generous) to those in need.
5. State of being.
6. Big.
7. Short for "identification."
9. Be _____ (kind) to someone.
10. _____ (retrieve) the groceries for your folks this week.
11. Huge.
12. Another state of being.
13. Say _____ (affirmative) when asked for a favor.
15. _____ (gather) food for the hungry.
17. Greasy substance.
20. More than one ark man.
22. _____ (pen) a letter to Grandma.
23. Honesty is a great _____ (distinguishing quality).
24. Invite a neighbor to a worship _____ (meeting).
27. Help clean up around the _____ (building for worship).
28. _____ (to make understandable) the Bible to someone.
31. Visit _____ (people who can't get around) Two words.
32. Powerful.
34. Roman numerals meaning "two."

40. Spanish for "one."
42. A E I _____.
44. A nice person _____ (minds) the request of others.
46. Spanish for "yes."
48. Invite a friend for _____ (noon meal).
49. Bull's eye.
51. "Leave it _____ Beaver."
52. Help _____ (organize) chairs for your youth minister. Two words.
53. Respect those of great _____ (years).
54. Help _____ (not in) around home.
56. Someone who digs.
57. Give your mom _____ (a peck). Two words.
59. To engrave.
60. " _____ Father, who art in heaven."
61. _____ West (Women's name).
62. _____ (give to another as well as to yourself) your candy bar.
64. _____ (prepare) dinner for your family.
67. Give your _____ (aged) clothes to a charity.
68. Short for "United Nations."
70. Short for "Nova Scotia."
71. Give a _____ (present) to a friend.
73. Lend money so someone can buy food to _____ (consume).
74. Collect a lot of these to raise money for your youth group.
76. All right.
78. "Give _____ that more may live."
79. Short for "Electrical Engineer."

For solution, see Answer Sheet, page 107.

Whoever turns a sinner away from his error will save him from death and cover over a multitude of sins.

(James 5:20)

If you're a Christian, it's because someone somewhere told you about Jesus. Now it's your turn to tell others. Does the idea scare you? What are some good ways to tell your friends about Jesus without looking like a geek?

The 64 squares on the next three pages contain all sorts of great—and not-so-great—ways to share your faith with others. Some of the squares contain Bible verses on the subject. As you read them during the game, you will learn some useful things about turning "a sinner away from his error." That's why we call this thing

- FOR TWO TO FOUR PLAYERS. (Or should we say "4-2-2-4 players"?)
- MATERIALS NEEDED: Scissors. Coins or other playing tokens, one for each player.
- INSTRUCTIONS:

1. Cut out all 64 squares. Shuffle and place them face down in an eight-by-eight square, like a chessboard.

2. Players each take a side of the game "board," as shown.

3. The row of squares nearest to a player is that player's "starting row." Each player puts his token on any square in his starting row.

4. The object of the game is to be first to reach the opposite edge of the board.

5. To begin play, the first player turns up whatever square his or her token is on and reads the square aloud. The token is moved according to the directions on the square. For example, if the square says "One right," the player puts the token on the square to the right. The player does *not* turn up the new square he lands on until the next turn.

6. Once a square is turned face up, it is left that way.

7. Two or more players may occupy the same square.

8. If a player lands on a square that is already turned up, the player immediately follows the directions on the square and keeps going until reaching an unused square.

9. If it is impossible to follow the directions on a square (for example, if the square says to move to the right and there are no squares on the right), then the player must return the token to the starting row and pick a new face-down square to begin on. The player must wait until the next turn before proceeding further. If all eight squares have been turned up, that player must use the second row, and so on.

10. What to do if a player gets trapped in a "paradox." An example of a paradox is shown here:

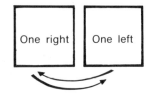

The player can't break out of this situation. The player must either start over on a new square in his starting row, or follow rule #11.

11. This is the rule that really makes this game fun and challenging! It may take practice to get it "wired."

    When it becomes a player's turn to turn up the square he is on, the player may instead choose any unoccupied square and exchange it for any other unoccupied square. There are three reasons a player might want to do this:

    1. To get out of a paradox.
    2. To put a "bad" square (such as "Start Over!" in front of an opponent in the hope that the opponent will land on it).
    3. To put a good square in his own path to increase the chances of moving ahead.

    Important: A square may never be exchanged two times in a row. A player must wait at least one turn before removing the square.

58

"Whoever turns a sinner away from his error will save him from death." (James 5:20) **Ahead one**	"The Holy Spirit will teach you . . . what you should say." (Luke 12:12) **Ahead one**	"I will tell of the kindnesses of the Lord." (Isaiah 63:7) **Ahead one**	God "wants all men to be saved." (1 Timothy 2:4) **Ahead one**
"How can they hear without someone preaching to them?" (Romans 10:14) **Ahead one**	"Therefore go and make disciples of all nations." (Matthew 28:19) **Ahead one**	"Make known among the nations what he has done." (1 Chronicles 16:8) **Ahead one**	Invite a friend to a fun youth group activity. **Ahead one**
Give someone a good Christian book. **Ahead one**	"Tell of all his wonderful acts." (1 Chronicles 16:9) **Ahead one**	Live your life in a Christlike manner. **Ahead one**	Do kind things for others. **Ahead one**
Start a lunchtime Bible study. **Ahead one**	Give a speech about Christ in speech class. **Ahead one**	Do an oral book report on a Christian book. **Ahead one**	Invite a Christian speaker (a good one) to a school assembly. **Ahead one**
Give an easy-to-understand New Testament to someone. **Ahead one**	Look for opportunities to talk about spiritual things. **Ahead one**	Visit people in the hospital. **Ahead one**	Answer questions from curious friends. **Ahead one**
Tell people about the fun stuff your youth group does. **Ahead two**	Write a letter about your faith to someone. **Ahead two**	Take friends to a good Christian concert. **Ahead two**	Give someone a good Christian album. **Left one**

"Let your light shine before men." (Matthew 5:16) **Left one**	"You are the light of the world." (Matthew 5:14) **Left one**	"Follow me," Jesus said, "and I will make you fishers of men." (Matthew 4:19) **Left one**	Stay away from sin. **Left one**
Play this game with a friend. **Left one**	Offer rides to youth group meetings. (Volunteer your mom if necessary!) **Left one**	Play a hot Christian album at the next party. **Left two**	Memorize verses about salvation and related topics. **Left two**
Write good Bible promises in your Bible's flyleaf for future reference. **Left two**	Ask God to give you opportunities to share. **Left two**	Ask God to teach you how to share effectively. **Right one**	Ask God to make you an influential Christian. **Right one**
Ask God to give your friends a curiosity about Him. **Right one**	Ask God to save someone you love. **Right one**	Keep praying for your friends for as long as it takes! **Right one**	Get to know the Bible well, so you can find verses when you need them. **Right one**
Volunteer to tell a good Bible story to the little kid's class at church. **Right one**	A lot of grocery stores sell Christian paperbacks. Encourage yours to do so. **Right two**	Give your older Christian books to your library. **Right two**	Talk to a visiting missionary about summer vacation missionary work. It's fun! **Right two**
Write a letter to the editor expressing a Christian viewpoint about items in the news. **Right two**	*Don't* throw gospel booklets out the car window! **Back one**	*Don't* scream the gospel through the school P.A. system without permission! **Back one**	*Don't* spray paint "God Rules!" on the auditorium! **Back one**

Don't hire sky writing airplanes!

Back one

Don't throw Bibles at passing bicyclists!

Back one

Don't tie gospel booklets to rocks and throw them through windows!

Back one

Don't carve "Jesus Saves" on your school desk!

Back one

Don't beat somebody up if he won't listen to your message!

Back one

Don't carry a sign that says "The World Ends Tonight!"

Back one

Don't wear a robe and stand on a mountain waiting for Jesus to return!

Back one

Don't eat garlic just before telling someone about Jesus!

Back two

Don't leave a gospel booklet *instead* of a tip at the restaurant! Waitresses *hate* this! (Leave the booklet *and* a 15% tip.)

Back two

Don't "TP" the local Krishna temple!

Back two

Don't be a "Sunday Christian!" Live for Jesus every day of the week!

Back two

START OVER!

START OVER!

START OVER!

START OVER!

START OVER!

Therefore, if anyone is in Christ, he is a new creation; the old has gone, the new has come!

———————— *(2 Corinthians 5:17)* ————————

This verse makes it clear that when a person becomes a Christian, profound changes begin to occur in his life. In fact, God does thousands of things for us. We can only talk about one of them in this game. . .but we say

 **ENOUGH!**

- ● FOR ONE PLAYER

- ● MATERIALS NEEDED: Pencil or pen (we suggest a felt pen).

- ● INSTRUCTIONS: We started to make a chart listing many of the things God has done for us. But as we were filling it in, we noticed a strange thing happening with some of the dots. They seemed to be forming an image! Connect the dots starting with #1 at the top left. The image will appear on the lower portion of the chart. Fold the top of the chart backwards along the bold line in the center of the chart.

NEW THINGS CHART

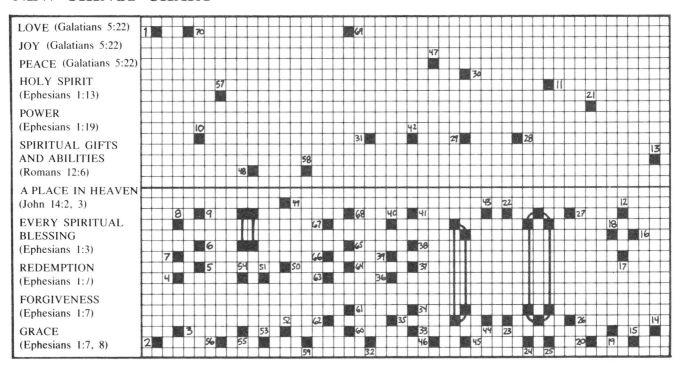

Now that you've played the game: Think about the word you've just discovered. It's important. It means that now, by God's power, you have the ability to accomplish things that non-Christians just cannot do. God has cut the ropes that tie you down to this world:

"It is for freedom that Christ has set us free. Stand firm, then, and do not let yourselves be burdened again by a yoke of slavery." (Galatians 5:1)

For solution, see Answer Sheet, page 106.

Then he said to them all: "If anyone would come after me, he must deny himself and take up his cross daily and follow me."

———————————— *(Luke 9:23)* ————————————

Sounds tough, doesn't it?!

You can get a hint *why* it's not always easy to be a Christian if you'll play this game we call

- FOR ONE PLAYER
- MATERIALS NEEDED: Pencil.
- INSTRUCTIONS: This is a hard version of the children's game known as a rebus—a word picture game. Here's an example in case you don't know how to play it:

Translation: Gold - l (God) Kiss -ks (is) glove - g (love) = God is love

For solution, see Answer Sheet, page 107.

Now that you've played the game: You see, Christianity is more than just a philosophy. A philosophy is a belief that you hold in your head. But when Jesus comes into your life, He makes sweeping changes and demands a revolution in your head, your heart, and your behavior!

Happily, Jesus gives us the power to live that high-powered Christian life. In fact, it's impossible to live it without His power!

"The Lord does not look at the things man looks at. Man looks at the outward appearance, but the Lord looks at the heart."

———————————— *(1 Samuel 16:7)* ————————————

That verse doesn't mean, of course, that God doesn't want us to *look* presentable. But what He's really concerned about is the condition of the heart. Even so, aren't most people you know more concerned about their outward looks than their inward conditions?

We call this game

LORD, I'M *GROSS!*

- FOR ONE OR MORE PLAYERS
- MATERIALS NEEDED: Scissors and pencil or pen.

INSTRUCTIONS: I know, I know—these instructions look long, right? But the game is really worth it!

1. Cut out the seven cards on the next page.

2. Read the phrase printed on each card. Choose one card with a subject you want to hear about and lay it to one side. (Six cards are about physical features like nose, teeth, and ears. One card is God's wisdom.)

3. Shuffle the remaining six cards and place them face up in three pairs, like this example:

       Pair A   Pair B   Pair C

4. We'll call them Pair A, Pair B, and Pair C. Look at Pair A. Do the colors of the eyes match (black or white)?

5. Look at Pair B. Do the eyes match? Look at Pair C. Do the eyes match?

6. Add up the number of pairs without matching eyes. You may have one matching pair, two matching pairs, three matching pairs, or *no* matching pairs. IMPORTANT: The pairs don't *have* to match!

7. Still with us? If not, read it again and figure it out. Now write down the number of matching pairs: 0, 1, 2, or 3.

8. Now follow steps 3 through 6 again (be sure to reshuffle), but this time look for matching expressions—smile or frown. When you've determined the number of matching pairs, write that number next to your first number.

9. Follow steps 3 through 6 one last time, but look for matching shirt colors. Write the number of matching pairs next to your other two numbers. You now have a three digit number, for example "312."

10. Look up that number in the "I'm Soooooo Gross!" list below. And there you have it! A helpful Bible verse or not-very-helpful comment that applies to the card you laid to one side! That comment applies only to that card, but there are several possible comments on the list for each card.

11. *Try it again!* Let your friends try it. Then make them explain how it works!

"I'M SOOOOOO GROSS!"

000 "Stop judging by mere appearances, and make a right judgment." John 7:24

001 Well, you can stand under it when it rains.

002 "All men are like grass, and all their glory is like the flowers of the field; the grass withers and the flowers fall." 1 Peter 1:24

003 Stand real close to an electric fan. Instant nose job!

010 "But blessed are. . .your ears because they hear." Matthew 13:16

011 Avoid pizza parlors. Someone might put cheese on your face.

012 " 'No more of this!' And he touched the man's ear and healed him" (Luke 22:51) Maybe it will happen again!

013 You could be a terrific connect-the-dots game.

Cut out these cards:

"My nose is TOO big."	"My big ears stick WAY out."	"My skin looks like a PIZZA."	"My teeth are GIGANTIC."	"My lips are HUGE."	"I have MANY problems."	God's wisdom about our appearance.

020 "Your beauty should not come from outward adornment. . . .Instead, it should be that of your inner self." 1 Peter 3:3, 4

021 Don't you wish you had a nose that big full of nickels? You'd be rich!

022 "Charm is deceptive and beauty is fleeting, but a woman who fears the Lord is to be praised." Proverbs 31:30

023 Hey, everybody blows it!

030 Become an elephant trainer. They'll think you're one of them!

031 Don't stand next to a cherry tree. Someone might pick your face.

032 Take hang glider lessons, without the hang glider.

033 It looks like a can of red paint sneezed on you.

100 Get a job opening paint cans with your teeth.

101 "Your belly is like a heap of wheat." Song of Songs 7:2 (NASB). Time to reduce!

102 Try a C-clamp.

103 Fat? You use a 30-inch belt—for a wristwatch band.

110 "A fool is consumed by his own lips." Ecclesiastes 10:12. So watch out!

112 "Truthful lips endure forever." Proverbs 12:19. Oh, no! Not *forever!*

120 With tusks like those, stay away from the elephant cage.

121 Your feet are too big? Go skiing without skis.

122 With that much ivory, you could build a piano.

123 Hard to find shoes your size? Use life rafts!

130 You could audition for the part of Donald Duck.

132 Take up tuba playing. Without the tuba.

200 "The Lord their God will save them on that day. . . .How attractive and beautiful they will be!" Zechariah 9:16, 17

201 Don't stand up in a restaurant. People might use your nose for a coat rack.

202 "We shall be like him, for we shall see him as he is." 1 John 3:2

203 You could be a great baseball star. And you wouldn't need a *bat!*

210 Avoid gusts of wind!

211 They say skin clears up as you grow older. Can you live that long?

212 Use one to carry your lunch in.

213 Next time, wring the grease out of the burger before you eat it.

220 "He has made everything beautiful in its time." Ecclesiastes 3:11

221 "Your nose is like the tower of Lebanon." Song of Songs 7:4. Now, *that's* a big nose!

222 "For the Lord takes pleasure in His people; He will beautify the afflicted ones with salvation." Psalm 149:4 (NASB)

223 Rent your nose out as a ski jump.

230 Play football: tie your ears to your shoulders for shoulder pads!

231 They say leopards change their spots. Maybe you can, too!

232 Don't stand too close to the waffle iron while your mom's cooking breakfast!

233 They say beauty is only skin deep. They don't know much, do they!

300 With teeth as crooked as yours, you could eat two sandwiches at once: yours and your *neighbor's!*

301 Chicken legs? Stay away from Colonel Sanders!

302 Rent yourself out as a beaver.

303 Skinny? Run around in the shower so you'll get wet.

310 Buy the *jumbo* size Chap Stick.

312 With lips like those, you don't need to wear turtlenecks.

320 Be careful if you bite your nails: you might lose an arm.

321 Skinny? Don't drink tomato juice. You might look like a thermometer.

322 With gaps like those, you could whistle three tunes at once!

323 Short? Comb your hair straight up and maybe no one will notice!

330 When you smile it looks like your head just caved in.

332 You don't need a pillow to sleep on at night. Use your lips.

Now that you've played the game: Our crazy game doesn't offer many answers for any appearance problems a person might have. But God does!

If you are concerned about your physical appearance, remember that God hears and answers prayers. He might not shrink your fat nose or reshape your ears, but He can easily give you a brand new heart—a heart full of warmth and cheer that will win you many good friends!

'Brothers, stop thinking like children. In regard to evil be infants, but in your thinking be adults."

———————— (1 Corinthians 14:20) ————————

How mature are you? Find out fast with the

☆ SPIRITUAL MATURITY RATE-O-METER! ☆

- ● FOR ONE OR MORE PLAYERS

- ● MATERIALS NEEDED: Pencil or pen.

INSTRUCTIONS: The Spiritual Maturity Rate-O-Meter is easy to use. Here's how: Starting at the bottom of the form with question #1, answer each question yes or no. Use your pencil or pen to follow the path of switches that your answers lead you on. The path will lead you higher and higher until you reach the top level. There you'll find your "Spiritual Maturity Rating!" Isn't science wonderful! If more than one person plays, you can compare your ratings. But you have to be honest!

Spiritual Maturity Rating:

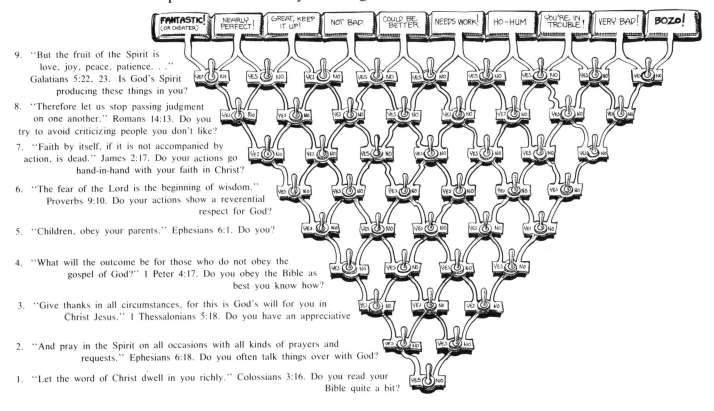

9. "But the fruit of the Spirit is love, joy, peace, patience. . ." Galatians 5:22, 23. Is God's Spirit producing these things in you?

8. "Therefore let us stop passing judgment on one another." Romans 14:13. Do you try to avoid criticizing people you don't like?

7. "Faith by itself, if it is not accompanied by action, is dead." James 2:17. Do your actions go hand-in-hand with your faith in Christ?

6. "The fear of the Lord is the beginning of wisdom." Proverbs 9:10. Do your actions show a reverential respect for God?

5. "Children, obey your parents." Ephesians 6:1. Do you?

4. "What will the outcome be for those who do not obey the gospel of God?" 1 Peter 4:17. Do you obey the Bible as best you know how?

3. "Give thanks in all circumstances, for this is God's will for you in Christ Jesus." 1 Thessalonians 5:18. Do you have an appreciative

2. "And pray in the Spirit on all occasions with all kinds of prayers and requests." Ephesians 6:18. Do you often talk things over with God?

1. "Let the word of Christ dwell in you richly." Colossians 3:16. Do you read your Bible quite a bit?

Now that you know your maturity condition: The nine questions on the Rate-O-Meter are a broad sampling of the sort of things a spiritually mature Christian will do. Making a habit of such things as Bible study, prayer, and obedience will make you a spiritually alive and growing Christian. It makes no difference how old you are!

71

"Finally, brothers, whatever is true, whatever is noble, whatever is right, whatever is pure, whatever is lovely, whatever is admirable—if anything is excellent or praiseworthy—think about such things." *(Philippians 4:8)*

Truth, honor, right, purity, loveliness, goodness, excellence, and praiseworthiness. Are these the sort of things your mind is normally filled with?

Unhappily, too many people tend to load down their minds with just the opposite. This game will encourage you to keep your head a bit tidier. So slip on your hip boots, grab a map, and play

GARBAGE, MAN!

- FOR TWO TO FOUR PLAYERS
- MATERIALS NEEDED: Scissors to cut out the player tokens, and a coin to toss.

INSTRUCTIONS:

1. Cut out and distribute one Head Token to each player.
2. Players put their heads—er, tokens, that is—on the starting line.
3. Each player takes turns moving his or her marker just one space each turn. (Always follow the direction arrows.)
4. When a player lands in a garbage can, the player flips a coin and follows the *heads* or *tails* directions as indicated by the coin.
5. The first player to cross the finish line is the winner. It can be harder than it looks.

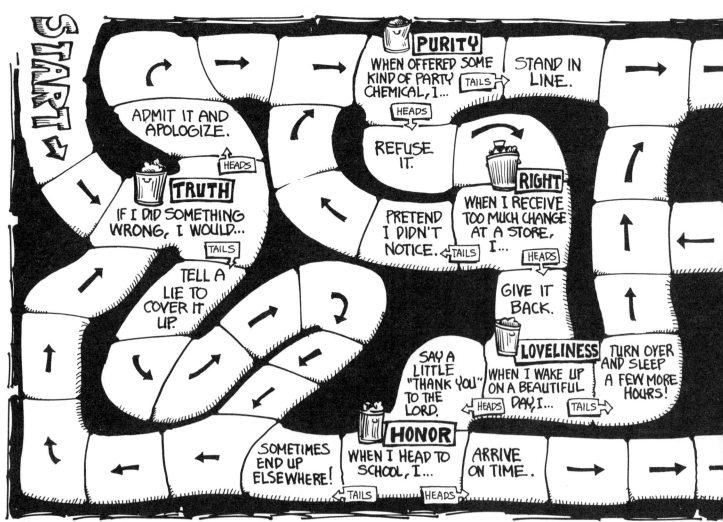

Head Tokens:

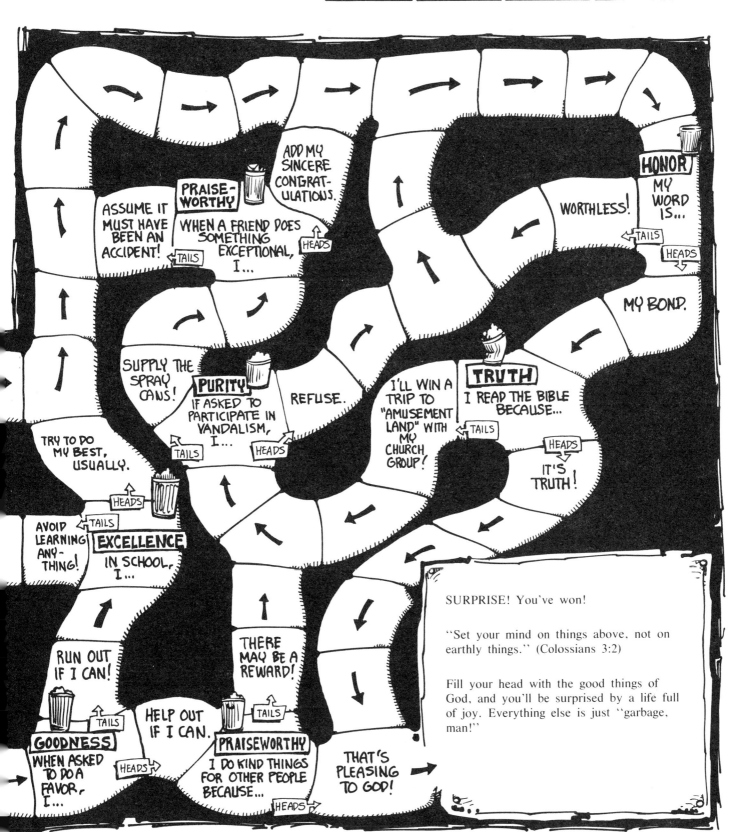

"Set your mind on things above, not on earthly things." *(Colossians 3:2)*

Where has your mind been lately? Set on God, or dragging in the dirt? Let's find out! Here is a set of ten simple situations. Compare yourself to them. Maybe you'll be

THE PERFECT TEN!

- FOR ONE PLAYER
- MATERIALS NEEDED: Pencil or pen.
- INSTRUCTIONS: Take a look at the situations below. Place a check mark in the box of each situation that honestly looks like something you'd do. Compare our answers to the "If You Checked. . ." sheet below.

If You Checked. . .

Box #1, you are probably a determined sort of person, disciplined, and tend to strive for personal excellence. If you carry this attitude over into your relationship with God, you will do well in life.

If you checked Box #2, you have revealed that you show little concern for others, and probably do not like people to have authority over you. You tend to have a hard time listening to God or following His word.

If you marked Box #3 or #4, you have little regard for honesty, and you probably don't obey your parents or others well.

#5 indicates that you enjoy spending time with God and with other Christians. You probably intend to do something with your life that has spiritual significance.

If you checked Box #6, you are dishonest and perhaps fearful or nervous. You may be incapable of handling responsibility.

If you checked #7 or #8, you show little self-control or patience. Your friendships will tend to be shallow and short.

Boxes #9 and #10 indicate that you are a kind person and have a high regard for others. You are probably not selfish or egotistical.

Are you a perfect 10? Probably not. But remember, set your mind on the things above and you'll be on the right track.

"He has showed you, O man, what is good."
———————————— (Micah 6:8) ————

What seems good to you? What are your important values in life? Friendships, happiness, world peace? Money, popularity, partying?

Your values are influenced by many things—parents, for instance, and teachers, and ministers, and music. But who or what should have the most influence in your life? Find out when you play

- FOR ONE OR TWO PLAYERS
- MATERIALS NEEDED: Pencil or pen.
- INSTRUCTIONS: The people in the center are each influenced by one of the objects scattered around them. When you carefully follow the lines to the objects, you can identify which person is tied to which object. (Some objects are tied to no one.)

Each time you connect a person to an object, take the first letter of that object and write it on the person. When the game is completed, the people will spell out the answer. Some of the objects are good influences, some are very bad. But the final answer is the best of all!

For two players: Take turns connecting lines. The first person to guess the completed answer is the winner.

For further study: Colossians 3:16; Philippians 4:8; Ephesians 5:1; James 1:22.

For solution, see Answer Sheet, page 108.

"Let the word of Christ dwell in you richly." *(Colossians 3:16)*

That verse simply means that we should let the Bible be our guide in life. Why? There are many reasons, but one of the best is that the Bible is God's Word, and God is a lot *smarter* than us!

He knows how we ought to live, and He knows what decisions we should make. His Word is like a series of sign posts that can guide us through life. All we have to do is follow instructions.

Hey, guess what! That sounds like a great idea for a game! We call it

YIELD!

Street Signs:

- FOR ONE OR MORE PLAYERS
- MATERIALS NEEDED: Scissors and pencil.
- INSTRUCTIONS: Your job is to drive your car all the way through the maze (which is much harder than it looks!) until you reach Heaven's Gates. Cut out all the street signs. By trial and error, place all the signs in the one and only correct order of the maze (we think!). There is just one rule: you must use all eight signs. You can play this alone or, by taking turns, with others. But plan to spend a long time. There are 40,320 possible combinations!

As you can see, life is a tangled weave! So let the Bible be your guide. Get to know the Bible. Stick your nose in it. Read it by yourself and attend Bible studies. And of course, *obey* it! In other words: YIELD!

For solution, see Answer Sheet, page 107.

Family living can be tough at times, but it can be fun, too, as you will see when you and your family play

FAMILY LIFE!

- FOR TWO TO FIVE FAMILY MEMBERS

- MATERIALS NEEDED: Scissors, cardboard, glue or tape, pencil.

- INSTRUCTIONS: *Every* family could stand some improvement. This game might even help! As you move around the game board, you'll find a few good ideas. You'll also find some bad things—with suggested solutions. Some of them might even be worth discussing after you play the game!

To play:

1. Cut out and assemble the spinner as shown. Or, if you prefer, use a numbered die to determine the number of moves a player makes.

2. Cut out and distribute the sets of Family Members, one set to each player.

3. Players take turns spinning spinner and moving Family Members along the game board, trying to reach the "Hey, You're Not So Bad After All!" house. Each player has only *one* Family Member on the board at a time. After one reaches the winner's house, then the player starts another Member. First player to put all four Members into the house is the winner—one big happy family!

4. Players follow instructions on the squares they land on. Squares may be occupied by more than one player at a time.

Glue or tape cardboard to back of the spinner. Poke pencil through center. Player spins spinner like a top. When it falls, the number *on top* shows the number of spaces to jump.

Family Members:

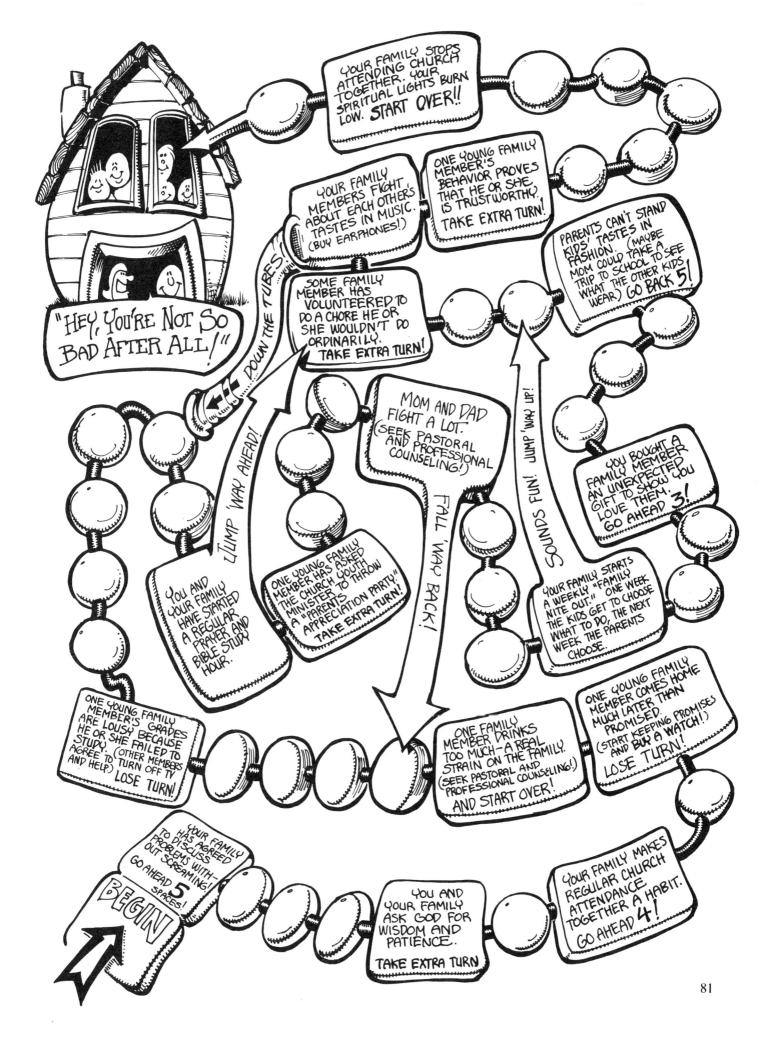

"Whoever can be trusted with very little can also be trusted with much."
————————————————————————— (Luke 16:10) ——————

How maturely do you act?

One of the best measures of maturity is the ability to handle responsibility. From the day you are "potty trained" to the day you pilot a 747, your maturity is gauged by how well you handle the job. The Bible verse above tells us that if we're in the habit of handling the small jobs well, we'll do fine with the big ones also.

Here's a nutty game that will give you some nutty ideas for jobs large and small to do around the house. We call it the

ALL-PURPOSE MATURITY CHECKER!

- FOR ONE OR MORE PLAYERS
- MATERIALS NEEDED: Scissors, two pencils and eraser, cardboard, glue or tape.

- INSTRUCTIONS:

1. Cut out and assemble the number wheel as shown.
2. Your job is to pick one phrase from each column below and put each phrase in the appropriate blanks in the sentence.
3. You do this by spinning the number wheel and letting it fall as shown. The number at the top will tell you which phrase to take from Column A to write in blank A. Spin the wheel a second time for Column B and again for Column C.
4. You have now filled in the sentence. Now you must do what it says! Good luck.

Glue or tape this spinner to cardboard. Jam the pencil through the center as shown. Spin the spinner like a top and let it fall. Whichever number is on top is the number of spaces to move.

"I (A) ——————— TO (B) ——————— THE (C) ———————."

Column A	Column B	Column C
1. promise	1. rinse out	1. bathtub
2. refuse	2. paint	2. bedroom ceiling
3. can't believe I have	3. vacuum	3. rug
4. wish I didn't have	4. mow	4. lawn
5. am mature enough	5. cook	5. dinner
6. am not mature enough	6. go to the store and buy	6. paper towels

Another great test of maturity level is the ability to realize that this game is not to be taken seriously!

There are lots of small but important things that a mature person will do without too much coaxing or complaining. You can judge your own level by checking your performance rating on these typical chores or habits:

Making your bed.
Cleaning up your messes.
Reasonable time to bed at night.

Reasonable time out of bed in the morning.
Good personal hygiene habits.

Kitchen duty.
Homework.

Well, the list goes on. Just remember, if God finds you faithful in the little dull things now, He will trust you with the big fun things later.

"Simply let your 'Yes' be 'Yes,' and your 'No,' 'No'; anything beyond this comes from the evil one."

──────── *(Matthew 5:37)* ────────

To help you understand what Jesus meant, play this game we call

WHAT'S **WRONG** WITH THIS GAME?

- FOR ONE OR MORE PLAYERS
- MATERIALS NEEDED: Pencil.
- INSTRUCTIONS: Circle or number or make note of all the things wrong with this picture.

You see, the picture just isn't accurate. The things you found just aren't true.

Likewise, as the Bible verse above points out, the picture you paint with your words and statements must be *accurate!* That's what Matthew 5:37 is saying. If you say you'll do something, do it. If you promise you won't, don't. Keep your promises. Be dependable.

For solution, see Answer Sheet, page 108.

"You are my friends if you do what I command. This is my command: Love each other." *(John 15:14, 17)*

How can you be the best friend your friends ever had? By showing them the kind of love that Jesus was talking about in those verses from the Gospel of John.

The maze below contains a lot of great things friends should be. Give it a go. We call it

✪THE ACME PALS PARTS DEPARTMENT!✪

- FOR ONE OR MORE PLAYERS
- MATERIALS NEEDED: Colored pencils, a different color for each player.
- INSTRUCTIONS: Little Earl has gone to the Acme Pals Parts Department Store to buy all the parts he needs to build a good friend. Help him find those parts. Starting at the door, find the route with the largest number of parts. End up at the cash register. Award yourself one point for each part you find. You can play alone or challenge a friend or two to beat your score. Compare your score to the chart below. There are two important rules:

  1. You can't cross your own path, except by using the stairs.
  2. You can't use the same segment of path twice. Of course, each player gets a turn to use all paths.

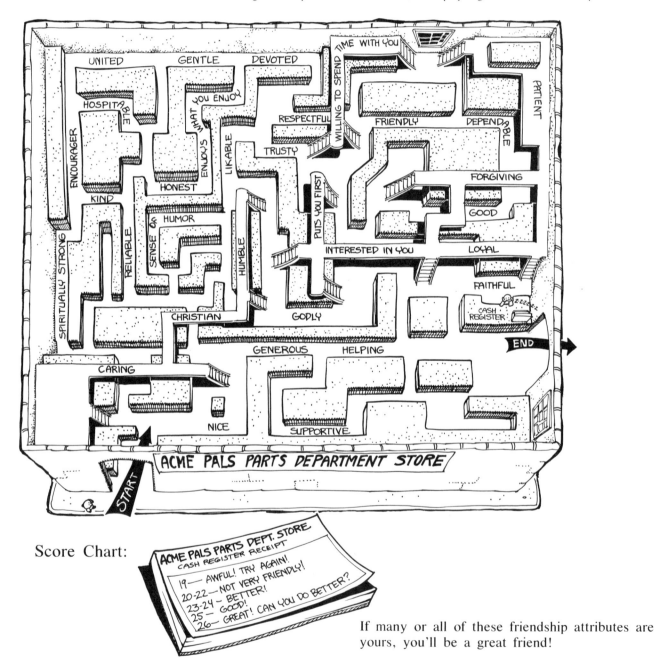

Score Chart:

ACME PALS PARTS DEPT. STORE
CASH REGISTER RECEIPT

19— AWFUL! TRY AGAIN!
20-22— NOT VERY FRIENDLY!
23-24— BETTER!
25— GOOD!
26— GREAT! CAN YOU DO BETTER?

If many or all of these friendship attributes are yours, you'll be a great friend!

THE FRIENDSHIP EXAM!

Surprise! This is a POP QUIZ! Let's find out how much you know about *friendship*.

- FOR ONE PLAYER
- MATERIALS NEEDED: Pencil or pen.
- INSTRUCTIONS: On the left side, I've listed a bunch of attributes that a good friend should have. On the right are the *original meanings* or *roots* of those attributes. Some are Old English, some are Latin, some are even Old Norse. Most are hundreds or thousands of years old. Your job is to draw a line from each word on the left to its proper meaning or root on the right. One is done for you as an example. You'll find that some are easy—and some impossible. Whatever the case, dust off your Old Norse and have fun!

ATTRIBUTES OF A GOOD FRIEND

Pal	Holpen (Old English)
Friend	Unus (Latin)
Chum	Bread sharer
Together	Camera room (Yep, that's right)
Supporter	To hang down
Helper	Brother (Gypsy) from "Bhratar" (Sanskrit)
Fond	Slang at old Oxford University for "chamberfellow" (roommate)
Dependent	To bring to
United	Used to mean foolish
Companion	Freond (Old English)
Comrade	Cyndelic (Old English); means natural
Kindly	Used to mean ignorant
Nice	Used to mean protection
Trust	Able
Strong	To gather
Devotion	Host or guest
Love	To confide in
Loyal	To look back
Concern	To suffer
Encouragement	Corpse
Faithful	Lufu (Old English)
Forgiving	Vow, or to give up
Generous	Means "in feelings"
Gentle	Together sift
Honest	Law
Hospitable	To give away
Humble	Of noble birth (Latin)
Sense of humor	Of noble birth (Old French)
Likable	Full of honor
Patient	Earth, ground
Respectful	To be moist

When you are done with the quiz, check your answers on the Answer Sheet, page 108. How'd you do? More importantly, how many of the attributes of friendship are yours? How good a friend are you?

"Two are better than one." *(Ecclesiastes 4:9)*

Everybody wants to have friends. Everybody would like to be popular.

This game might give you a few tips on things to do and things to avoid in your quest to find friends. We call it

A LARGE CIRCLE OF FRIENDS!

- FOR TWO TO FOUR PLAYERS
- MATERIAL NEEDED: Scissors to cut out cards and token, coin to flip.
- INSTRUCTIONS:

1. Cut out all the Friend Cards and the Players' Tokens. Give each player seven Friend Cards and one token. Put the remaining Friend Cards in a pile, which will be the "bank."

2. Player with Token #1 goes first. He flips the coin to see how many spaces to move his token: one space for "heads," two spaces for "tails."

3. Players follow the instructions on the squares they land on. When a square says "Take a Friend Card," that means to take one card from *each* player. When a square says "Lose a Friend Card," that means the player must give one card to *each* of the other players. Squares may be occupied by more than one player.

4. If a player runs out of cards, he must start over. Because that player has no cards, other players can collect instead from the bank.

5. The object of the game is to be the first to land in "A Large Circle of Friends." In order to do so, a player must have at least ten Friend Cards.

P.S. This game can take much longer to win than you think!

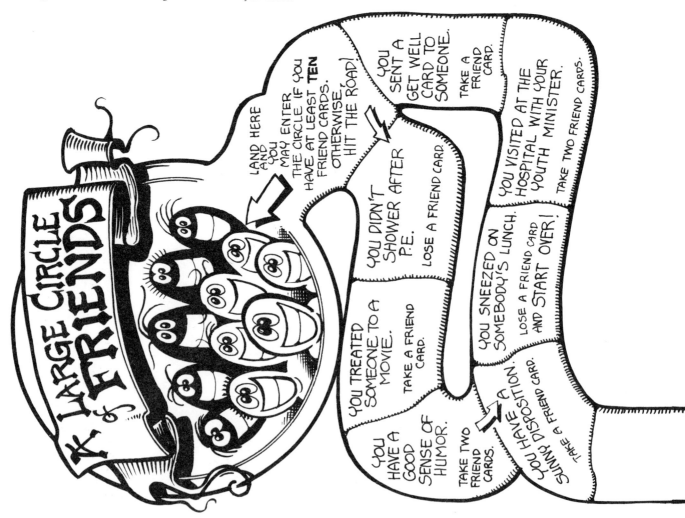

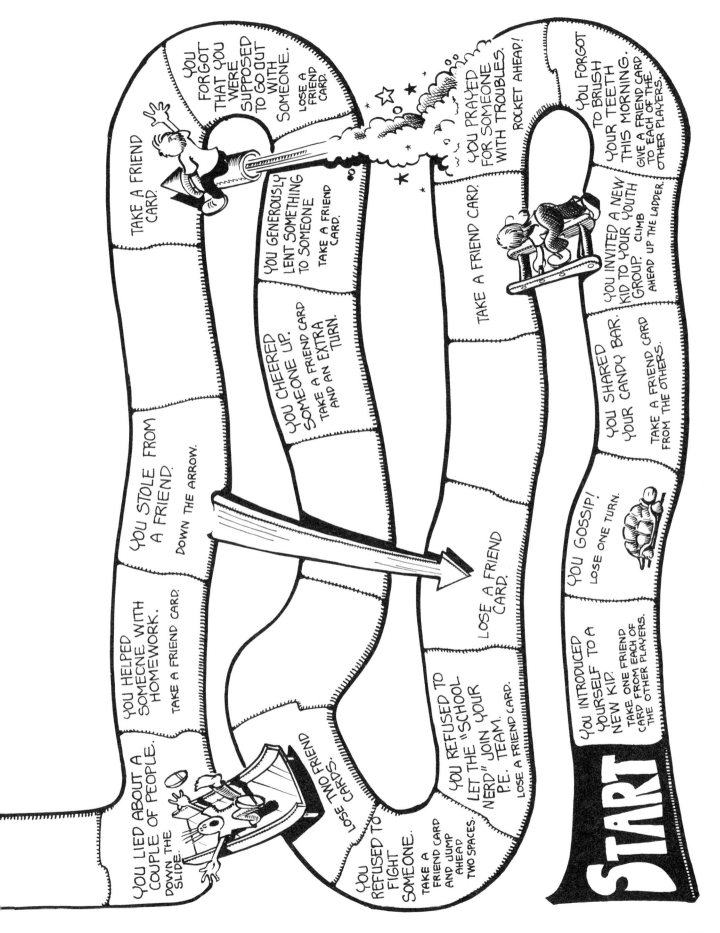

89

Friend Cards and Players' Tokens:

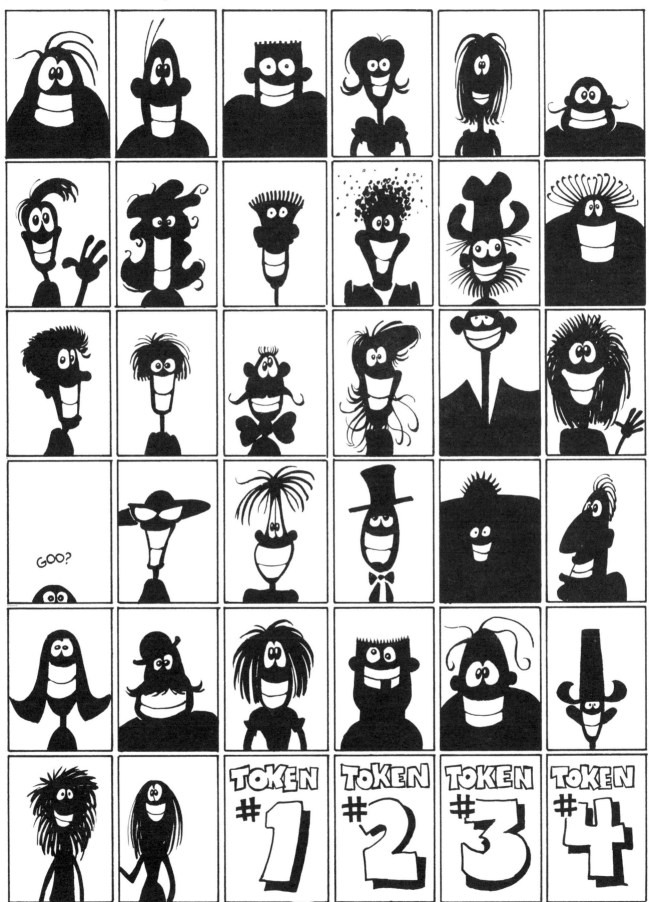

 "Love is patient, love is kind. It does not envy."

———————— *(1 Corinthians 13:4)* ————————

You are probably familiar with I Corinthians 13—the "Love Chapter," as it is called. It's famous because love is such a popular topic. But long before you fall in love with someone. . .you have your dreaded FIRST DATE.

Dating. What sort of things do *you* look for in a dating partner? Let's find out. Try the

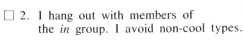 GREAT DATE DEBATE!

- FOR ONE PLAYER
- MATERIALS NEEDED: Pencil or pen.
- INSTRUCTIONS: Study all the situations pictured below. Check off only the ones you strongly agree with. Then compare your answers to the "Blind Date" sheet below.

☐ 1. A person's physical attractiveness is the most important thing.

☐ 2. I hang out with members of the *in* group. I avoid non-cool types.

☐ 3. I tend to form long-term dating relationships only with Christians.

☐ 5. I like a date with a sense of humor.

☐ 4. I date people who have the hottest cars or biggest pools or things like that.

☐ 6. I expect the person I date to date no one else.

☐ 7. I want someone who will do what I want to do, not someone who'll make me do boring stuff.

☐ 8. I drop someone like a rock if they don't treat me with respect and consideration.

☐ 9. I'd rather date a person with a great report card than a poor report card.

Blind Date Rating Sheet

IF YOU CHECKED	
Box #1:	You're probably just starting your dating life (junior-high-age, right?) You still care more about your own wants than your date's.
Box #2:	You sound insecure. Your relationships probably don't last long.
Box #3:	You're starting out on the right foot. Keep up the good work! But be careful not to become a "Christian snob."
Box #4:	You care more about yourself than you do the other. Also, you're missing a lot of good friendships!
Box #5:	You're probably a steady, dependable person. You form strong relationships centered on the personality of the other.
Box #6:	You're the faithful, loyal type—or you're jealous!
Box #7:	Sorry, but that sounds pretty self-centered. When you do find someone you truly like, you may not know how to act.
Box #8:	You're smart! Chances are you won't end up married to a violent or mean person.
Box #9:	You tend to surround yourself with winners. Keep it up and you won't be a loser.

Now that you've taken the test: How'd you do? Are you a blind date, or do you date wisely, with your eyes wide open?

Just remember one thing—every dating relationship you form should include *three* people: you, your date, and God!

Making the most of your time, for the days are evil.

———————————— (Ephesians 5:16, NASB) ———————

As Christians, it is our responsibility to wrestle time from Satan's hands and give it to God. In other words, as much as possible, our days should be focused on God.

Here's a great way to figure out how much time you already give to the Lord—and the more the better, because

------------EVERY SECOND COUNTS!--------------

- • FOR ONE PLAYER
- • MATERIALS NEEDED: Pencil or pen.
- • INSTRUCTIONS: The chart below represents an average week in your life. Fill out the approximate number of hours you spend each day doing the things listed in the column at left. Each day's activities should add up to exactly twenty-four hours.

	MONDAY	TUESDAY	WEDNESDAY	THURSDAY	FRIDAY	SATURDAY	SUNDAY
Sleeping							
Eating (All meals)							
TV, radio, and other forms of passive (spectator) entertainment.							
Sports, games, and other forms of active entertainment.							
School (include travel to and from)							
Homework							
Chores you normally do							
Job (include travel to and from)							
Hanging around with friends							
Reading for pleasure							
Personal prayer							
Personal Bible study							
Church Bible studies and worship services							
Church prayer meetings							
Other church related stuff							
Anything else you can think of (list)							
TOTAL HOURS							

We hope you learn *two* important things from this exercise. One, there's a good chance you spend only a few of the 168 hours a week that God has given you with God! Two—there's no good reason the time you spend at work, at school, and so on can't be spent with God. Keep your thoughts on Him. Let Him be with you as you move through each day.

P.S. If you had trouble limiting each day's activities to only twenty-four hours, now you know why you have a hard time getting things done!

Jesus said: "If you have not been trustworthy in handling worldly wealth, who will trust you with true riches?"
The Pharisees, who loved money, heard all this and were sneering at Jesus.

—————————————————————————— (Luke 16:11, 14) ——————————

Even two thousand years ago people loved money more than they loved God!

You may not have pockets full of loot, but what you do have can be spent wisely or foolishly—as you probably discovered the first time you wasted a buck on cotton candy!

This little game contains eighteen suggestions for wise ways to spend your money. You'll find some things to buy or do for yourself, and some for others. The words are not all easy to find—they twist, turn, and even go backwards! So see if you can straighten out

DOLLAR$ AND SENSE!

- FOR ONE PLAYER

- MATERIALS NEEDED: Pencil or pen.

- INSTRUCTIONS: Find these phrases in the dollar sign, and draw circles around them.

1. Get an easy-to-read Bible for a friend.
2. Put some in the collection plate.
3. Give an unexpected gift.
4. Send a greeting card to grandma.
5. Charity.
6. Buy a good Christian book.
7. Treat your folks to a meal.
8. Help support a missionary.
9. Save for a church outing.
10. Get equipment for youth group.
11. Treat a new kid after church.
12. Buy a Christian album.
13. Buy flowers for a patient.
14. Lend snack money.
15. Attend a Christian concert.
16. Get a Christian magazine subscription.
17. Contribute to hunger relief.
18. Save up for camp.

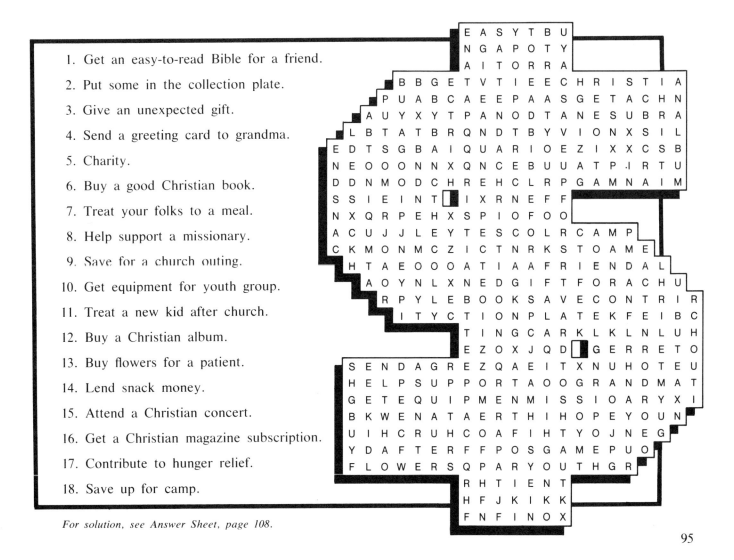

For solution, see Answer Sheet, page 108.

"Who has woe? Who has sorrow? Who has strife? Who has complaints? Who has needless bruises? Who has bloodshot eyes? Those who linger over wine."

——————————————————————— (Proverbs 23:29, 30) ———————

Drugs and alcohol. We've all been told to beware. We all know the damage they can cause— to other people. But many people just can't see the writing on the wall. "Not us," they say. "One shot won't hurt us!" But when they're wrong, they often end up against that wall.

Can *you* see the writing on the wall? On our wall below is an easily recognizable piece of information that pertains to the dangers of substance abuse, as you can clearly see. Or can you? Give it a try. Play

ON THE WALL!

- FOR ONE OR MORE PLAYERS
- NO MATERIALS NEEDED

INSTRUCTIONS: Just like we said, it's on the wall.

Now that you have played the game: The "writing" on the wall indicates danger. Substance abuse is self-abuse. Respect yourself: stay healthy.

For solution, see Answer Sheet, page 108.

Therefore each of you must put off falsehood and speak truthfully to his neighbor.

Honesty is one of the evidences that Christ is real in your life, for Jesus is the God of truth.

The Word of God (the Bible) is truth (see John 17:17). If you want to be an honest and truthful person, it makes sense to focus your life on God and His Word.

Here's a silly game with no real purpose except to remind you that the Bible is the real source of truth, and that if you want to know the truth, you must spend time learning the Bible.

We call it  *Bible* BENDERS

- FOR ONE OR TWO PLAYERS

- MATERIALS NEEDED: none.

- INSTRUCTIONS: Below is a list of familiar and not-so-familiar quotations. Your job is to decide which ones are from the Bible, and which are not.

Two can play this game: One player looks at the answers and then announces which quotations are from the Bible—but he doesn't necessarily have to tell the truth! The other player tries to guess, for each quotation, whether the first player is telling the truth.

1. "Cleanliness is next to godliness."
2. "God helps those who help themselves."
3. "A mighty fortress is our God."
4. "Idle hands are the devil's tools."
5. "Two heads are better than one."
6. "Rock and roll is here to stay."
7. "Misery loves company."
8. "Honesty is the best policy."
9. "A mind is a terrible thing to waste."
10. "Cheaters never prosper."
11. "My breath is offensive to my wife."
12. "Everybody tells little white lies."
13. "Do one to others as they do one to you."
14. "All that glitters is not gold."

For solution, see Answer Sheet, page 108.

"But I tell you that men will have to give account
on the day of judgment for every careless word they have spoken."

──────────────── (Matthew 12:36) ────────────────

Do you have a problem with bad language? Your problem may be worse than you think, because bad language is more than just swear words. It also involves gossiping, flattering for the sake of gain, telling lies, being negative all the time, and so on.

This game involves several Bible verses that discuss the positive and negative aspects of our language. They reveal that careless words come from the heart (the personality), that we should be bearers of good news, that we should use our breath to praise God, that—well, you'll find out when you play

GOT THE **CONNECTION?**

- FOR ONE PLAYER
- MATERIALS NEEDED: Pencil and eraser.
- INSTRUCTIONS: Little Earl has had a bit of an accident, as you can see. Your assignment is to help the doctors reconnect the eight body parts with each part's original position. You must not cross your own path, except by "bridge", or use the same segment of vein twice! Because if you do, Little Earl may end up talking with his ear!

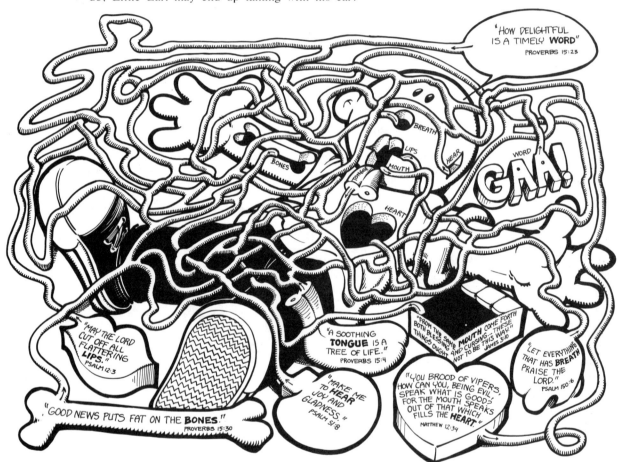

Now that you've played the game: Remember to watch your language. Keep in mind these two verses:

"The tongue of the righteous is as choice silver." (Proverbs 10:20)

"The tongue of the wise brings healing."(Proverbs 12:18)

Got the connection?

For solution, see Answer Sheet, page 109.

Do you not know that your body is a temple of the Holy Spirit, who is in you, whom you have received from God? You are not your own; you were bought at a price. Therefore honor God with your body.   *(1 Corinthians 6:19, 20)*

Our bods are God's. He expects us to take care of them. This means that we should not only avoid unhealthy habits like smoking and running across the airport runway, but we must do things that are *good* for our health.

Here's a nutsy game that will give you some tongue-in-cheek exercise ideas. We call it

WADS OF FUN ENDURANCE EXERCISES!

- FOR ONE OR TWO PLAYERS
- MATERIALS NEEDED: Drinking straws and spit wads—or regular dartboard darts—tape or tacks to stick this game to the wall.
- INSTRUCTIONS: Hang this page on a board or wall. Every morning or evening fire a dart or spit wad at it. Perform whatever exercise you are unlucky enough to hit.

For two players: Aim at the most distasteful exercises. The other player has to do them! Take turns until you collapse.

Well, OK. This wasn't such a great game. But let it serve to remind you that God is to be glorified by our bodies—the way we use them and the way we care for them. Exercise and eat right. And wads of wuck!

Humble yourselves, therefore, under God's mighty hand, that he may lift you up in due time. Cast all your anxiety upon him because he cares for you. *(1 Peter 5:6, 7)*

This game is all-out, cutthroat competition. In order to win, you must be aggressive, quick, and a little bit mean. That's why we call it

DIRTY DOG!

- FOR TWO PLAYERS
- MATERIALS NEEDED: Two pencils of different color.
- INSTRUCTIONS: The rules are simple. Each player puts his or her pencil on the appropriate "Start" area. At a signal to begin, they race their pencils through the maze toward the "Success!" sign. First one there wins.

Your pencil's path cannot cross your opponent's pencil path, except by bridge. So it pays to be a dirty dog—in other words, you increase your chances for a win if you try to block the other player's path whenever possible. Ready? GO!

Now that you've played the game: In a humorous way, this game reflects the attitude of a lot of people in this world. They aggressively and meanly race through life knocking people out of the way in an attempt to achieve as much so-called success as they possibly can.

The Bible verses at the top of the page, 1 Peter 5:6, 7, is the exact opposite of this sad attitude. It says that God will insure our true success—if we humbly live our life for Him now. For some reason, that tremendous promise from God seems to be a well-kept secret.

But now *you* know it. Now you know the secret of success.

GET THE **PICTURE?**

- FOR ONE PLAYER

- MATERIALS NEEDED: Pencil or pen.

God is the source of real happiness! In the picture game below is hidden one of the great promises in the Bible—a promise about happiness. You played games like this when you were a little kid, but in case you've forgotten how, follow the example shown:

Translation: Gold - 1 (God) kiss - ks (is) glove - g (love) = "God is love."

If you worked the game correctly, you found Psalm 37:4—one of the greatest promises in the Bible. It means that if you make God the center of your life, He in turn will reward your heartfelt desires. That's the way to true happiness in life: to be close to God.

For solution, see Answer Sheet, page 109.

ANSWER SHEETS

S.O.S.!

(There may be more than one solution.)

BIBLES AND BUBBLES

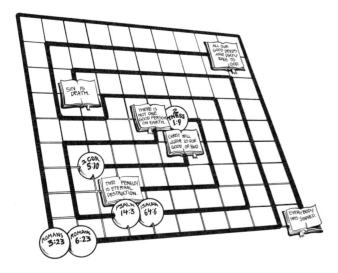

THE KEY TO THE KINGDOM

WHO DO YOU THINK HE IS?

Wock: Word (John 1:14) and Rock (1 Corinthians 10:4).

Counth: Counselor (Isaiah 9:6) and Truth (John 14:6).

Waiator: Way (John 14:6) and Mediator (Hebrews 12:24). A mediator is a "go-between."

Shephet: Shepherd (John 10:11) and Prophet (Matthew 21:11).

Lormb: Lord (Luke 2:11) and Lamb (John 1:29).

Messselor: Messiah (John 1:41) and Counselor (Isaiah 9:6). The Messiah is the "One sent from God."

Dong: Door (John 10:9) and King (Luke 23:38).

Roy: Rock (1 Corinthians 10:4) and Way (John 14:6).

Lird: Life (John 14:6) and Word (John 1:14).

Savod: Saviour (Luke 2:11) and God (Isaiah 9:6).

Propiour: Prophet (Matthew 21:11) and Saviour (Luke 2:11).

Mediah: Mediator (Hebrews 12:24) and Messiah (John 1:41). A mediator is one who settles arguments.

Laght: Lamb (John 1:29) and Light (John 8:12).

Lid: Light (John 8:12) and Lord (Luke 2:11).

Gherd: God (Isaiah 9:6) and Shepherd (John 10:11).

Trufe: Truth (John 14:6) and Life (John 14:6).

Kior: King (Luke 23:38) and Door (John 10:9).

WORD JAM

```
B E N E V O L E N T B C M N C C F R I E N D Z
X O B A L M I G H T Y Y I N C O R P O R E A L
G J M P E A C E O F L G D K E G R E A T I S C R
L U X N J Q K Z L A O R I P P P A V T C E E
O D S P I R I T Y T V O A V N M M E T F G W
R I G Q I K P H M O H E D A A X I G N R O H A
I E R N R G R S T E T E R N A L N E Z U S R
O A X V K H J E Z R Q J H G T H T E Z T S B D
U Y T O S M M X J L E J I S S P E R F E C T L E
S L I V I N G H U I W N Q S I E E E Q R O H S R
T F G B T F A S G X Q T N K O N N P C O E S W
U U X L B W U T H Y J M Q J K N K P Y W S I
P O W E R F U L T Z O R I G H T E O U S S D E
```

The answers can be found in the Bible verses listed below. The more difficult terms are defined.

Spirit (John 4:24). In this case, the Bible means that God is much more than flesh and blood.

Holy (John 17:11). Here, God is called "Pure," meaning without sin.

Righteous (John 17:25). Means holy, pure, and just or fair.

Omniscience (Matthew 10:30 gives an example of the word, which means "to know everything.")

Corporeal (Luke 24:39). Flesh and blood. The significance is that God, through Jesus, became an actual human being, able to experience and understand human problems.

WORD JAM (Continued)

Omnipotent (Matthew 19:26 gives an example. The word means "having all power.")

Omnipresent (Psalm 139:7-12 gives an example. It means that God is everywhere.)

Benevolent (Matthew 5:45). Kindly and good.

Rewarder (Hebrews 11:6). He rewards us.

One (Deuteronomy 6:4). There is one God.

Creator (1 Peter 4:19).

Almighty (Matthew 19:26).

Judge (2 Timothy 4:8).

Father (Romans 1:7).

Perfect (Matthew 5:48).

Truth (John 3:33).

Mercy (Ephesians 2:4).

Glorious (Revelation 7:12).

Blessed (Revelation 7:12).

Wise (Revelation 7:12).

Powerful (Revelation 7:12).

Friend (James 2:23).

Just (Psalm 49:14).

Divine (2 Peter 1:4).

Eternal (Genesis 21:33).

Invisible (Romans 1:20).

Living (Matthew 16:16).

Good (Mark 10:18).

Love (1 John 4:8).

Great (Titus 2:13).

King (1 Timothy 1:17).

Light (1 John 1:5).

Peace (Philippians 4:9).

CHRIST'S WORD PUZZLES!

BIBLE STARS!

(Some may have more than one solution.)

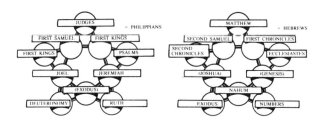

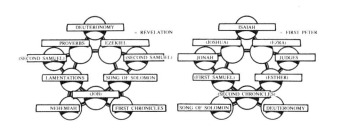

GOD'S WORD PUZZLE

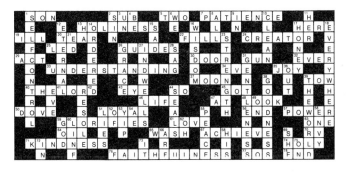

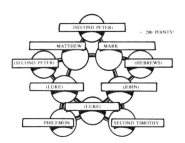

THE CHURCH SEARCH!

```
B L O O V E T O P U R I F Y B E L I E V E R S
I B F E L L O W S H I P T O E N C O U R A G E
O R B T O H E L P I T S M E M B E R S E E A A
D I U X O Y V O R S E G I B T Y E A I E V T L
U N I T Y M A V A N O R B L O T H Y M N E H L
G G L M I E N I I A N D T O D E E D P D R U T
B B D L T O G L O R I F Y G O D O N R U Y R O
T E I W O S E R V I C E T O G O D A O R O E L
T L N S Y O L E A R L Y J E O I F N V B M T O
O I G E E N I T O B E O R N O A I D E Y E O V
A E U N T X Z R U N N I K T D X X T O M A N E
J V P B H I E T H E C O M M U N I T Y G A V B
E E I C H R I S T I A N E D U C A T I O N B B
S R N L O V E U N I F I E E D O R B I L L O T
I S T O M A T U R I T Y J E S U Z O Y O U R T
```

PEOPLE ARE PUZZLING!

LOADS OF CODES!

Worm - m + k (Work) *the* mallard - L - lard + zeppelin - ppelin (maze).

Reel - el + ad (Read) *the* letters cone - ce (on) *the* projector - jecter + pear - a (proper) P + bathtub - btub (path) = = "Work the maze. Read the letters on the proper path."

The proper maze path reads: "Circle every third letter in the paragraph below."

And I was showing fear. But I was not so we rose. Can I taste the hair? I believe. Eat the cod.

The paragraph's decoded message is "A is one B is two C is three etc." This is a reference to the simple numbered alphabet code used in children's games.

The crossword puzzle code, therefore, is:

Not a dog
Not a frog
For the head
Not skinny
Share
Not nine
Baseball stick
Male kid
Not a cat
Don't sit on a _____
Not cold
Not two
Not walk
Wet dirt
Not out
Catch fish
Finished!

Thus, the final answer is: "To have another mind."

A PUZZLING GOD?

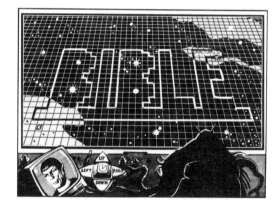

WHERE THERE'S A WILL, THERE'S A WAY!

DOT'S ENOUGH!

CROSS WORD PUZZLE!

V	I	S	I	T	S		G				I		H	I		I	N		G
O		U		A		B	I	B	L	E	S	T	U	D	Y		I	C	E
L		F	O	R	G	I	V	E					G		E	P	C	O	T
U	N	F	I	T		G	E		W	I	T	N	E	S	S		E	L	
N	O	E	L		C				R		R			E		E		L	
T	A	R			H	O	S	P	I	T	A	L		R	O	X	I	E	
E	H			A	U		H	O	T		I			V		P	I	C	K
E	S	A	U		R	O	U	T	E		T	H	R	I	L	L		T	
R			N		C	U	T	E		S		E		C		A			
	C	L	O	T	H		I	N	V	I	T	E		E		I		S	
A		U		A		O	N	T			O	D	D		A	N	G	E	R
G	E	N	E	R	O	U	S		M	S		S	I	C	K			T	
E	T	C		G	U	T		O	A	H	U		G	O	I	N	G	U	P
	C	H	E	E	R		C	L	E	A	N		G	O	S	S	I	P	
O	H		A	T		S	A	D		R		E	E	K	S		F		
K		A	T		S	O	N		F	E	V	E	R			S	T	A	Y

YIELD!

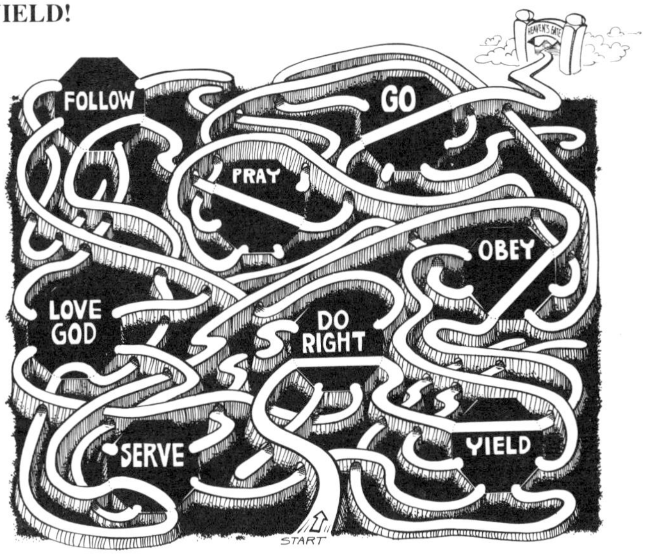

PICTURE THIS!

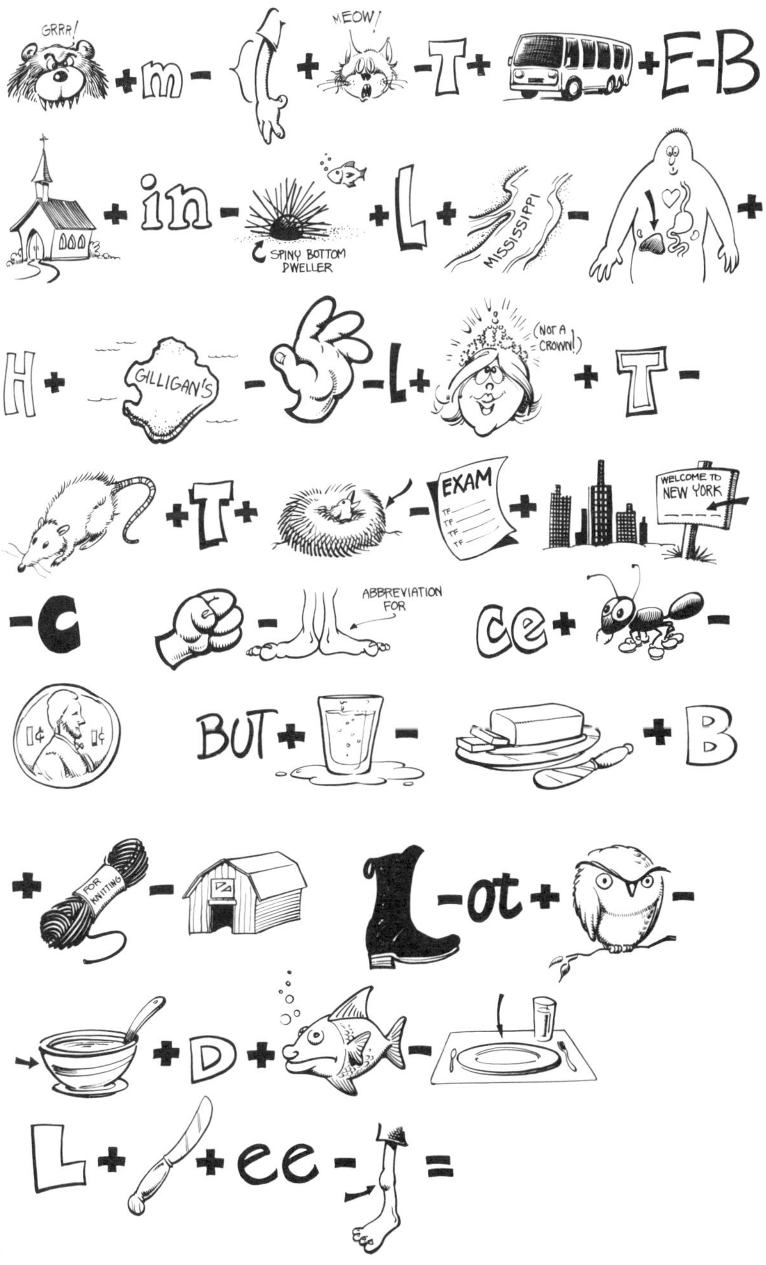

Bear + m - arm + cat - t + bus + e - b = Because

Church + in - urchin + L + river - liver + h + island - hand - L + tiara + t - rat + t + nest - test + city - c = Christianity

Fist - ft = is

Ce + ant - cent = a

But + water - butter + b + yarn - barn = way

Boot - ot + owl - bowl + d + fish - dish = of

L + knife + ee - knee = Life.

"Because Christianity is a way of life."

NO STRINGS ATTACHED!

BIBLE BENDERS!

Only #11 is from the Bible: Job 19:17!

THE FRIENDSHIP EXAM!

Don't worry, this was a tough one! But maybe you've learned that there's more to friendship than just sitting with someone in the cafeteria. Friendship should include all of the attributes you saw in the game!

ATTRIBUTES OF A GOOD FRIEND

Pal
Friend
Chum
Together
Supporter
Helper
Fond
Dependent
United
Companion
Comrade
Kindly
Nice
Trust
Strong
Devotion
Love
Loyal
Concern
Encouragement
Faithful
Forgiving
Generous
Gentle
Honest
Hospitable
Humble
Sense of humor
Likable
Patient
Respectful

Holpen (Old English)
Unus (Latin)
Bread sharer
Camera room (Yep, that's right)
To hang down
Brother (Gypsy) from "Bhratar" (Sanskrit)
Slang at old Oxford University for "chamberfellow" (roommate)
To bring to
Used to mean foolish
Freond (Old English)
Cyndelic (Old English); means natural
Used to mean ignorant
Used to mean protection
Able
To gather
Host or guest
To confide in
To look back
To suffer
Corpse
Lufu (Old English)
Vow, or to give up
Means "in feelings"
Together sift
Law
To give away
Of noble birth (Latin)
Of noble birth (Old French)
Full of honor
Earth, ground
To be moist

The answers are from *Macmillan Contemporary Dictionary*, Macmillan Publishing Co., Inc., and *Webster's New Twentieth Century Dictionary, Unabridged Second Edition*, Simon and Schuster, New York.

WHAT'S WRONG WITH THIS GAME?

Clock is numbered backwards. Calendar's days and dates are wrong, and no month ends in "ley." Slipper in toaster. Wall switch upside down. Left window's curtains hung upside down. Right window's curtains hung outside. Crescent moon has star in impossible spot. Two flags are blowing opposite directions. Airplane flying backwards. Parachute upside down. Boy in window across street is sideways. "1600 Pennsylvania Ave., Washington D.C." is the address of the White House. Tire truck has square tires. Mirror store sign is backwards. Most "OPEN" signs aren't sorry about it. Man on bus stop is upside down. Kid is riding his tricycle in the busy street. Bus is on sidewalk. Bus and tire truck are going the wrong way on a one way street. Fork in flower vase. Cereal box opened at both ends. Fork in bowl on cereal box. Square egg on plate. Liquid in glass is at strange angle. Pencil has two erasers. Coffee is coming out of the wrong part of the pot. Pot held by a hand with six fingers. Coffee being poured into upside down cup. Newspaper weather forecast predicts sunshine at night.

ON THE WALL!

DOLLARS AND SENSE!

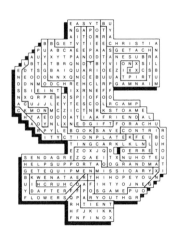

GOT THE CONNECTION?

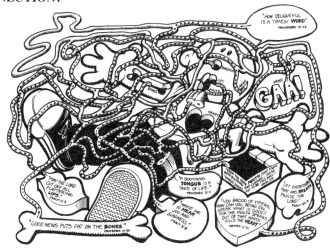

GET THE PICTURE?

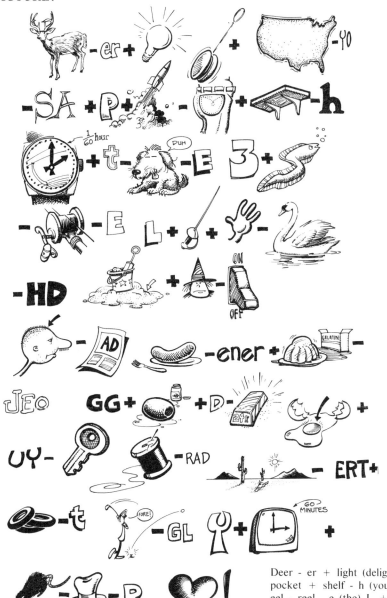

Deer - er + light (delight) yoyo + USA - SA + p + rocket - pocket + shelf - h (yourself) minute + t - mutt - e (in) three + eel - reel - e (the) L + sword + hand - swan - hd (Lord) sand + witch - switch (and) head - ad (he) weiner - ener + Jello - jeo (will) gg + olive + d - gold (give) yoke + uy - key (you) thread - rad (the) desert - ert + tires - t (desires) golf - gl (of) y + hour + rat - hat - r (your) heart! ``Delight yourself in the Lord and He will give you the desires of your heart!''

INDEX of Scripture Verses

Verses are listed in the order they appear in the Bible. Each verse is followed by the game number—in bold print—in which the verse is featured. The contents page at the beginning of this book lists the games by number and title.